C0-AQZ-237

GETTING More Family Out of Your Dollar

James E. Kilgore, Ph.D

Getting More Family Out of Your Dollar
Published by Yawn's Publishing
210 East Main Street
Canton, GA 30114
www.yawnsbooks.com

This book is an updated edition. The original was first published in 1978.

Library of Congress Control Number: 2012952348

ISBN: 978-1-936815-64-7
978-1-936815-65-4 e-book

Printed in the United States.

DEDICATION

With thanks to all the families from whom I have learned these lessons in the last fifty years

CONTENTS

INTRODUCTION

"No, it's too expensive," the shopper said as she made a judgment about the value of an item the store offered. The worth of the product was not great enough for her to pay the price.

"I don't care what it costs, give her the best treatment available!" To this anxious husband worried about the condition of his seriously ill wife, cost was secondary to the priceless recovery of his beloved.

"What more can I do? I've given them the best of everything." This troubled father had discovered that money was not a guarantee to the happiness and adjustment of his children.

Each of these statements shares three things in common-money, relationships, and human judgment. The problem is keeping all three in proper balance. Many a juggler drops one or more of these elements in his act on the stage of human development.

The special focus of this book is to look at these three elements as they relate to life within the family. We will consider some of the causes of our money failures, as well as some potential directions for success in getting more family living out of the use of money. How your family uses or abuses its money may well determine its success or failure in constructive relationships. Money attitudes serve as one of the best barometers of the atmosphere in relationships.

We will develop some very practical helps for breaking the vicious cycles of defeat and depression that often surround our money problems. Patterns will be developed that will strengthen the bond of togetherness and do away with the destructive weapons of criticism and retaliation that erode the very fiber of marriage and family relationships.

The final section of the book contains materials to help you use this book in creative ways within your family, within a small group of other parents, special classes within your church or Sunday school, or any other special study group. We hope this will be helpful in a variety of ways.

There is a satisfaction to be discovered only when you can be free of the shackles of money and transform it into a source for experiencing security and fulfillment. Hopefully, the positive directions offered here will help you start that happy process of getting more family out of your dollar.

James Kilgore
Canton, Georgia

PART ONE

MONEY REFLECTIONS

"The man who knows right from wrong and has good judgment and common sense is happier than the man who is immensely rich! For such wisdom is far more valuable than precious jewels. Nothing else compares with it."

ONE

IMPROVING FAMILY LIFE IS IT POSSIBLE WITHOUT MORE MONEY?

"HAPPY ARE THOSE WHO DREAM DREAMS AND ARE READY TO PAY THE PRICE TO MAKE THEM COME TRUE."

More family is not necessarily the result of more money!

As a marriage and family counselor, countless couples have said to me: "We were so happy in the beginning. We didn't have much, but we had each other. The more we got, the more we spent. Now we have enough money, but somewhere along the way we lost our happiness."

We can't blame money for our failures nor can we credit our relationship successes to it either. How happy we are does not depend on what we have! But that's easy to say, it's not easy to put into practice. Within most of us is buried the idea that more money equals more happiness. How did it get there? Subtly!

Advertising is designed to communicate and to convince. Persuasion is at its very heart. A competent promotion campaign creates within the consumer a desire to buy, invest, own, or improve something. As a psychologist I am interested in why this occurs. I am curious about the pull of advertising on my finances.

Part of the financial fantasy created by advertising is the belief that quantity equals quality - *more is better.* But it isn't.

John put his head in his hands and sobbed. Joyce sat there and fumed. He felt despair and she seemed angry. They were filing for bankruptcy. Their attorney had referred them to me. Their debts were staggering and their resources were very limited, yet they were both talented and attractive people. I listened carefully to their story.

Success had come quickly. John had risen in his firm until he had "nowhere to go that was up." Joyce had helped him finish his graduate degree and then began having children. He became more and more absorbed in his job; she became a compulsive mother. They both wanted the best for their family. They bought a lovely home, two cars, then a boat, a second home at the beach, and a family membership in the country club. When John started his own business, they entertained more and more. Very little time was left for the family. But they had convinced themselves that more gadgets, more toys, and more money would solve their problems. They borrowed and borrowed again in the face of a sagging economy. Finally, they could borrow no more.

John felt he was a failure and Joyce was angry and embarrassed. They tried to cut back on things, but to no avail. Bankruptcy seemed inevitable.

Fortunately, even a bleak story like this can have a positive conclusion. John and Joyce began a new chapter of family living by first learning some new principles about the meaning of the word "more". And second, by placing their relationship to themselves and their children prior to their financial goals, they changed the direction of their value orientation.

John and Joyce learned four "more" principles. The same principles they learned can apply to your family. Here they are:

"More" Principle No.1:

Your goal for "more" IS the family not the dollar!

Getting more family out of your dollar is the goal-not getting more dollars from your family. Intimacy and sharing take precedent over investments and shopping. People - especially the members of your family - rank higher than *any* project. Getting more relationship through your use of money is more important than getting more money through your relationships.

"More" Principle No.2:

Values are learned more powerfully in family interaction than in any other learning situation.

You are your children's model on how to use money.

They will learn more by watching you than by listening to

you. Our priorities help us to make proper decisions about money. The earlier we learn these priorities, the easier it is to live by them as we grow. Families teach more effectively and affect more permanently our values and priorities than any other institution in the world.

"More" Principle No.3:

The more effectively I manage money the more money I have to use.

As we mature, self-control increases. The control of our resources is an expression of that maturity. Learning basic steps in money management helps me mature and provides more choices for me. As I act responsibly with my resources, I experience more freedom in my decisions.

"More" Principle No.4:

When money is used for more effective relational living, it brings more pleasure to life!

The more wisely I use my resources the more satisfied and fulfilled I am. The greater my satisfaction the fewer tensions emotionally and physically, and the less I am controlled by circumstances. Only the man who learns to give away what he possesses can be free of its shackles. A relationship exists between value and management. The higher my priorities about people the more significant my financial decision will be, but in a corresponding way there will be greater satisfaction from the use of my resources.

These "more" principles, if applied consistently, can bring you more emotional security and satisfaction in the use of your money.

I want my children to learn all of these lessons from me, because I think I can be a more effective teacher than any other financial agency in their world. It is probably harder for children to learn from parents and harder for parents to teach children than it is for the teacher who has more emotional distance from their pupils. But that does not keep me from the challenge or the opportunity of trying to teach my own children.

One of the ways that I have tried to communicate with my children at significant moments in their lives is by letter writing. These letters tend to summarize what we have experienced with each other, and often help me to express succinctly some of the things which we have struggled with in our experiences together. The following is a letter which I wrote to my son in thinking about his going away to college:

Dear Jim:

Too soon your car will be pulling out of the driveway for the trip to college and a new opportunity in your maturity.

When I was in college, the story went that sons wrote to their fathers with this message: "Dear Dad. No mon. No fun. Your Son. " And the story went on that Dad answered with this curt response: "Dear Son. So sad. Too bad. Your Dad." I'm sure you'll have some money needs while you're away at college, but I hope our correspondence will be a little bit more complete than that example.

Since I am supposed to be something of a communications specialist, I decided there were a few things I wanted to summarize before you went to college. You might say these are the things I have tried to say to you verbally and nonverbally over the last 17 years.

First, I want to say again that I am proud of you. From that moment in the hospital nursery to this moment the continuous thread of our experiences has been that pride. It has been woven through our high moments of sheer pleasure and our low times of painful conflict. That pride underlies all the other feelings when I see a smile on your face or hear the words, “Thanks, Dad.” It is the pride that reminds me that you are my first born. I've tried to make it a two-way street - remembering that sons need to be proud of their fathers too. I hope you'll be governed by that pride while you are away from us. I've often thought twice about my actions because of what your anticipated reactions might be. We share names, first and last. Help me be as proud of what people see and feel when they identify you as my son as I hope you are when people know that I am your father.

If you're at all like your namesake, you'll probably feel like choosing a permanent life partner while you are in college. From the first day I saw your mother on our campus, her life has become intricately woven into mine. During these nearly 20 years together we have deepened our dependence upon each other and increased our love. There are many' 'secrets” to a good relationship. I guess our secrets are that we enjoy being together, that we really care about each other, and that we have certain basic things in life on which we agree. One of the most important ones is our faith. I've shared the beginnings of your faith with you. I was even fortunate enough to have the privilege of baptizing you - something many fathers can never share with their sons. But it is likely that you will share this deeper experience of a growing faith more fully with your life partner. Take your time in developing that kind of relationship and intimacy. There is no greater joy than the satisfying love between a man and a woman who are deeply committed to each other, and no wounds are more painful than those inflicted by lovers. You have only one body; choose carefully with whom you share it.

You are going into a different phase of money management when you leave home. I tried to share with you about money with our first visit to the bank with your savings account, through allowances, your car and learning how to manage it, our loans, and many other ways. You've worked hard each year to learn to use your money wisely. Your career choices will affect the amount of money you will have later, but I'll do the best I can to help you appreciate things in these years. That means that I'll help to support you through college, but you'll still have to earn your way through college - not just academically but also partially financially. I think we'll both be happier with that arrangement. In any case I'll stand by you, both as your financial and as your emotional partner. I have done well in my profession, and I enjoy that. I want you to gain the kind of skills that will be just as satisfying for you in whatever career choices you make. Money will not bring you happiness, but the way you use it will.

As we mature together, I'll look forward to your "answer" to my letter in written and living form. Enjoy these last times in high school and keep enjoying your progress through college. Enjoy where you have been, but not enough to keep you from where you are going. I hope this period in your life will have enough satisfactions to keep you happy, enough challenges to keep you alert, enough pain to keep you tender, and enough uncertainty to keep you dependent on God.

I love you,

Dad

Your ideas and interests in life may differ greatly from those expressed in this book. Our hope is that by examining these suggestions, they will serve as a catalyst for thinking and discussion in your family.

You ***can*** get more family out of your dollar!

TWO

YOUR MONEY TALKS - WHAT DOES IT SAY?

"A GOOD REPUTATION IS MORE VALUABLE THAN MONEY." Publilius Syrus

"A GOOD REPUTATION IS MORE VALUABLE THAN THE MOST EXPENSIVE PERFUME."
Eccl. 7: 1 The Living Bible

MISER MIRRORS

"He squeezes a nickel until the Indian's feathers fall out," a friend once said of his colleague. His reputation as a miser followed him from unappreciated employees to tip less service person to his own children, but Mr. Miser never saw himself as others did. Like the queen who expected her mirror to say, "You are the fairest of them all," he expected people to see him as generous but the way he used his money told another tale.

Have you ever considered how your money talks about you? It may not only say what your priorities are, but also tell how you go about achieving them.

A person who "hoards" money abuses it. Money is an instrument -of exchange. In itself it is basically worthless, but it is valued by our vesting worth in it. The question comes, why would one hold on to money? One answer is that he believes having is as important, if not more important, than being. His claim to worth is in the value, power, or desirability of what he has, not who he is. Reward is in gaining things, not growing, feeling, or increasing awareness.

What makes a miser? What are the kinds of experiences that lead to a hoarding experience? Your best friend may not tell you, but these guidelines could.

Childhood deprivation is a contributor to this money disease. It breeds an insecurity that is based on the fear of not having something important. The feeling of an insufficient supply in the face of demand breeds anxiety.

A man who has grown up in the depression will often abhor the feeling of being "poor." Being hungry or sensing that he is "less" than a fellow human being because of the absence of some possession or amount of money is a situation that he wants to avoid.

A good friend of mine grew up in an area characterized by racial discrimination. His family made money, but they were unable to buy a home in the particular neighborhood of their choice. As an expression of an alternate choice of investment, his family purchased an expensive automobile. For his family, the Cadillac was an alternative to a nicer home. However, as an adult, he developed an almost opulent pattern in a choice of home and furnishings. By knowing this friend you would understand that his background was partially responsible for the kind of life style he chose as an adult.

We learn the hard way that having things doesn't always change our feelings about them. Satisfaction is not found in quantity.

Mary was a young, attractive airline employee. She made a good salary, had a savings account, lived in a nice apartment, dressed well, and drove a new car. But Mary was a worrier. The first thing she said to me was, “I can't afford to come to a psychiatrist too many times.” I carefully explained to her that among several major differences between psychologists and psychiatrists was the fact that psychologists are usually less expensive in their fees. While that temporarily assured Mary, the question of money came up numerous times during our sessions. I learned that Mary came from a wealthy but conservative family. While growing up, the first question she encountered about any interest was, “How much will it cost?” In some children rebellion breeds irresponsibility. Had Mary been this way, she too may have developed an “I don't care what it costs” attitude. Being a first born - and most of them seek very hard to please their parents - Mary adopted the attitude and style of her parents. Her first question regularly was, “How much?”

As Mary learned that pleasure was not always measured in cost, she also began to invest her money in things she enjoyed. Sometimes she found that enjoyment came through the cost and not in spite of it. Her family had missed much of the joy of their wealth by “hoarding” it and failing to use it. Fortunately, Mary gained new insight that led to new behavior on her part.

The three basic insights she learned were:

1. *Money possesses no intrinsic security.*

Mary had enough money, but she felt insecure. When she gained freedom in the use of money, she also discovered a greater security.

2. *Security in judgment about money only comes through some personal risk and satisfaction.*

Mary found that she had to accept the responsibility of money before she could experience the freedom to decide if she liked the way she used it.

3. *Being controlled by money is just as prison-like as being controlled by an actual guard.*

She made these mistakes before marriage. Undoubtedly, she will teach her children a different lesson about the use of resources than she learned.

Since I'm interested in *why* things happen, let me suggest how Mary may have learned these "lessons." Consider where there may be parallels in your family. A family teaches by words, examples or by omissions within its system. What parents say, how parents spend and what parents don't say or buy teaches children about the use of money. All of this gets complicated when the parents have conflicts about the use of their funds.

In Mary's mind were the phrases she had heard about money. "A fool and his money are soon parted." "Money is the root of all evil," and "A bird in the hand is worth two in the bush!" If these sound familiar, the mentally recorded messages of your parents or early influential adults may also follow in this negative vein.

Is it true that a wise man *has* his money? Mary questioned that - so do I. I believe a wise man knows his resources, applies them well and enjoys their benefits. He may possess things that are representative of his wealth. Some of these things may be valued in dollars. My monetary belief system says that a wise man knows how to use his money and is free to do so.

No man is free of the shackles of what he possesses until he can give it away. An ancient Hebrew proverb says, "It is possible to give away and become richer! It is also possible to hold on too tightly and lose everything."

Like Mary, many of us *learn* platitudes that will not stand the test of human experience. Sometimes these unreasonable ideas create stress or discomfort within us in the handling of our money. It is not really the amount I have to spend which is important. It is the attitude I have about spending it.

My relationships are shaped by these attitudes when I am young and they continue to shape my relationships when I am older. Mary's attitudes often limited her relationships. Early in her life "more" principle no. 1 had been violated. Mary was taught or "caught" the idea that having money was a goal. In her case that goal preceded having relationships. The goal all of us want to teach our children is that the use of our resources should increase the level of intimacy in family interchange and that family members are not valued by the amounts of money which they produce or which they consume. Later we'll examine how one goes about teaching the "more" principles to their children.

THREE

YOUR PATTERNS GUIDE – HOW DO THEY LEAD?

"IF YOU MUST CHOOSE, TAKE A GOOD NAME RATHER THAN GREAT RICHES; FOR TO BE HELD IN LOVING ESTEEM IS BETTER THAN SILVER AND GOLD."

Henry Ford was once asked, "How much money does it take to satisfy a man?" He answered, "Just a little bit more." It was a curious but cryptic insight into human nature.

YOU ARE A TEACHER!

To teach our children anything we must first have learned it ourselves. Some parents appear to be natural teachers. Others may have to work at it. But we all are teachers. In money matters, it is essential to remember that not having a lot of money does not disqualify a parent from teaching about the use of money. All parents teach lessons about money. Rich parents may be poor teachers; financially poor (momentarily) ones may be rich educators.

I teach by the philosophy I have about money. I demonstrate that philosophy by my practice of saving, spending, and sharing my resources in life. That's the test of my philosophy. If you cannot readily identify your philosophy of money, consider how each of these three tests works in your life - *saving, spending, and sharing.*

SAVING

Planning for the future is inherent in a savings program. Good, regular savings patterns reflect a disciplined way of life. Your philosophy of saving may tell you much about yourself. How do you save? Where do you save? Why do you save? What do you save?

Savers are disciplined futurists - people who want to be ready for what is coming up. It may be a vacation, Christmas expenses, retirement, or a major expense item like a car, a boat, a house, etc. Some saving can be for the proverbial "rainy" day.

We teach our children about saving through our saving habits. When my children were three, five and seven we opened savings accounts at the local bank in our small community. Each week or two we regularly went to the bank together to deposit nickels and dimes. It was not as important as some of the larger savings accounts the teller handled but she treated the children with the same courtesy she showed to the larger depositors. As a result saving became a regular and pleasant experience for the children.

Ten years later my, then 13 year old saved enough money from lawn work and other small jobs to upgrade the quality of trail bike he got for Christmas. His saving period covered nine months of regular trips to the bank on his own. He was one of the few "drive-in" window customers on a bicycle! I believe there was a connection between his persistent efforts and the earlier saving habit we established years before.

Saving reflects the value I place on something I want. It may also reflect an attitude about when I am ready to spend money. Borrowing is an important financial function to which we devote attention later. Whatever the goal of the saver, however, a special satisfaction comes with being able to draw from an account and pay for an item without financing it.

A bank, a savings and loan association, or other financial institutions may be good places to save. Another helpful institution for many of us is a credit union. I find a special sense of belonging to an institution which in some measure I own. More than fifty years ago I joined a Credit Union. I have regularly saved and borrowed through it advantageously over that period of time.

A part of my ongoing education is to learn to use many different kinds of financial agencies and resources. Families can share learning experiences together by visiting financial institutions and becoming acquainted with the services offered. A personal relationship with a financial advisor is an important asset in a crisis time. It is much easier to establish this kind of relationship on a non-emergency basis. The advice of that person "'feels" better if your relationship has been one of some duration.

HABITS THAT MODEL

The saving habits of parents are models for their children.

Spending patterns also become examples for our children. These values are "caught" more than taught in families. We observed the values placed on people relationships, relationships to things, and relationships to powers.

Emergencies often teach us to re-examine our values. The ongoing pursuit of those values may make a more lasting impact. In hospitals or doctors' offices we think more in terms of people than prices. Because of this the physician stands in a powerfully significant spot. Some of my medical friends resent this responsibility. I observe that most families perform above average in physical crises. Where we often fail is in the emotional crises. The further we get from any crisis the more careless we become.

SPENDING

The careless use of money is powerful model for our children. I need to ask myself; how do I spend my money? Where do I spend my money? For what do I spend my money? Why do I spend it? When I answer these questions I can get a picture of my spending profile.

Here's an experiment in self-analysis. Take your checkbook and list all your checks for the past three months. You may simply want to layout your cancelled checks in separate piles according to various expenses. Add up the cancelled checks in each separate pile. Add up the several categories-rent for house payments plus utilities, telephone, etc., to get your shelter cost. Do the same for food, clothing, installment debt, savings, contributions or charities, investments, etc. What you see will begin to be a mirror of your values. It is important to remember all the "automatic deductions" for taxes, payments, etc. which may not be easily visible.

That may sound a little "old fashioned" for those who do electronic banking. You can print a three month list of expenditures and deposits from your computer (or simply follow it on line). Your e-bill payments will be reflective. The method will be the only thing that changes.

What do you see in this pattern? You should be able to learn something about yourself. Whatever you learn in this experiment is probably being learned by your family. They see what you see as you look in this mirror.

Now you can make important commitments to change what you dislike about your spending patterns. In six months most of us can bring about great transformations. The most common problem is the abuse of credit. Our chapter on plastic power has some practical suggestions for this.

What is crucial here is the question of values. What you do, not what you say, is where your values are. Push yourself to determine which changes you want to make. Then begin to rank them by priority and set calendar goals for accomplishing the changes. Spending patterns model for our children, but they can be controlled and modified by careful management and planning.

SHARING

Some years ago I made a significant personal discovery about money. What I give away often brings me more pleasure than what I keep. It is not what I hold but how I use what I have that enriches my life. Joy is investing in those things that can bring a return. Money works like that too. The discipline of careful use provides the freedom to spend happily and to give generously in all areas of financial life

Here is a lesson in the Hebrew concept of tithing. In the early days of Israel, each family brought to the tabernacle 10 % of its productivity. Theoretically, each 10 families could support a priest at the same level of existence that they each shared. It was a survival and support plan for the Levitical (priestly) system.

In the early days of Christianity, a form of communal living was first attempted. However, as the movement grew, a "storehouse tithe" was adopted much like the "temple tax" of Judaism. This is an appropriate survival mechanism for churches, but the concept of sharing resources is even broader than percentage giving to a local congregation.

Sharing, which teaches our children, is more a perspective about money. Money is a useful resource for the accomplishment of our goals-nothing more or less. We must all reach a minimum survival level for comfort. The level of happiness about money is beyond that - when the meaning of my values can be translated into sharing with others.

RICH RETURNS

A Jewish physician I know gives two months each year to a Christian mission hospital in some part of the world. He pays all his expenses and receives no compensation for his services. Yet he talks more of the surgery he has done "for nothing" in Africa than the delicate operations in America which have brought him professional fame. His "return" on the investment of himself in those mission situations is far more meaningful than the satisfaction of several thousands of dollars, presumably his return for some of the surgery he has done here in the United States.

A teenager who invested $10 a month in a high school

student through the International Family Foundation program later told me how good she felt each time she exchanged letters with her Korean pen pal. She "sacrificed" some things from her life, but she gained far more from what she shared. Some time ago I established a creativity ministry award at my alma mater, to recognize ministers who found inventive ways to apply the skills of the ministry. One recipient's address to the student body of young seminarians was worth the entire program. His expression of appreciation and the encouragement of his creative efforts in the ministry made my efforts in establishing the program extremely rewarding for me.

Different meanings come from giving as compared to making money. Both meanings are important, but making money without giving and sharing is missing one of the greatest joys one can know.

Our children learned some of this by "adopting" a sister in Indonesia and a little brother in Korea. Through exchanges of correspondence and pictures, all of us "stretched ourselves" across the seas to include another world in our hearts. The supreme use of money is sharing it with others-in your family and by enlarging your family to include the world.

Our early experiences in sharing led to an expanded awareness of our world and how it could be touched. This process gave birth to the International Family Foundation, an organization now reaching families around the world. If you are just beginning to deal with the use of your resources, start with your own family first, but don't stop there. There is a world family to share with, too!

1.Information about the program of the International Family Foundation may be obtained by writing IFF, Suite 220, 1558 Marietta Highway, Canton, Georgia 30114.Online: internationfamily.org or e-mail: jekiff@hotmail.com.

PART TWO

FAMILY RELATIONSHIPS

"THE FOOL WHO PROVOKES HIS FAMILY TO ANGER AND RESENTMENT WILL FINALLY HAVE NOTHING WORTHWHILE LEFT. HE SHALL BE THE SERVANT OF A WISER MAN."

Proverbs 11: 29 The Living Bible

"IT IS BETTER TO EAT SOUP WITH SOMEONE YOU LOVE THAN STEAK WITH SOMEONE YOU HATE."

Proverbs 15: 17 The Living Bible

FOUR

FAMILY INTERACTION LESSONS

"TEACH A CHILD TO CHOOSE THE RIGHT PATH, AND WHEN HE IS OLDER, HE WILL REMAIN UPON IT."

Proverbs 22 : 6 The Living Bible

We have seen that the most significant lessons about money can be taught best in the home. The family has seven unique educational advantages as an educational center. They are:

1. The family does the *earliest* teaching of the child.

2. The family has the *greatest* amount of time to invest in the child.

3. The family is the *most likely* source of love and acceptance for its members.

4. The family has *greater latitude* for individuality than any other societal institution.

5. The family gives more *life centered* education.

6. The family provides a *team* of teachers.

7. The family is a *continuing* adult education experience.

PERSONAL REFLECTIONS

You can easily see the parallel applications to financial learning in each of these points. You give your child his first lessons about money. Some psychologists would even suggest that the earliest perceptions are the most lasting ones. Try it on yourself. Can you remember when you first learned something about money? Be careful not to stop too soon. Linger for a moment on grade school experiences, and perhaps you can remember something in the preschool time of life. Perhaps something one of your parents did or said about money will come into your mind. First, remember the experience and then reflect on what you learned from it. Next, see if you can determine what part of your present behavior is affected by this incident or lesson. These early learning experiences have tremendous significance for most of us.

TEACHING TIME

The family can teach children more lessons about money simply because there are more hours in which to teach. How hard it is to check the indulgence allowed us by our parents and grandparents! Nursery school educators and grade school teachers often see the kind of values which have been instilled or missed in children by how students handle the materials provided for them. The family, particularly the mother, has the most time with the child. Siblings also play an important part in the total teaching time as well as grandparents. Feelings, more than facts, are most often communicated in the family.

The strong influence of those feelings may lead to developing stable, rational money-habit patterns. Or the sensed, or "caught" rather than taught, communications may encourage an irrational base for handling money.

ROOM TO GROW

In the first 5 years of life, most basic values are learned. These years are almost exclusively devoted to the family education process. I may choose to augment my child's education with TV as "entertainment" but I am still choosing a learning pattern for him.

Families can allow us to make mistakes about money too. Some of the lessons are learned the hard way. One of the most difficult lessons my youngest son, Jeff, ever learned about money came on his 8th or 9th birthday. We had moved to a new home in Georgia and one of his grandparents had sent him some money rather than mailing him a gift. Jeff went shopping and wanted to carry his own money-which I recall to be about $10 or $11 - in his own wallet. We reluctantly agreed. As we shopped, he laid his wallet down to "try out" a prospective purchase. Neither his mother nor I realized it until we got to the checkout line and asked where his money was. It was a sad little boy who searched the aisles unable to find his "lost" wallet. I don't remember his shedding tears outwardly. I doubt that I did either. But I think both Daddy and son cried inwardly about going home empty-handed. We both learned something about care in handling money and the struggles for independence in doing so. "Lost money" provided a time for comfort and solace in the family rather than indulgence by simply buying the toy anyway. There was another time for the toy, but this occasion for learning in our relationship occurred only once. In the family we love and accept each other, even in the face of money mistakes. This "latitude," which the family allows, is very important.

I can also recall a lot time spent waiting for shopping decisions to be made. But each child had to have some attention while making his choice. Only a parent or a grandparent possesses the patience to wait for a child to "choose" the toy within his money limits on a shopping trip.

Much of our learning about money takes place in the market place where we negotiate with each other without the privacy and protection of our homes. Perhaps that is what "life-centered" education really means. The grocery store, the shopping mall, and the pet shop become our teaching centers rather than the classroom.

TEAM TEACHING

Then there are the lessons which the team teaches. Dad, Mom, and the other brothers and sisters all get in on the act. Not all agree. Sometimes Mom and Dad disagree. Many times the older sibling passes along his information on how to "handle" the parents in some situations. One can learn some interesting things about himself by overhearing his children's' conversations. I remember once hearing one of my children say, "Dad would never do that." You can bet that I was unpredictable when the request was finally brought to me.

Not all the lessons that either children or parents learn are pleasant. Some family conferences reveal surprises for the parents and remind us that we still have much to learn. But remember "more" principle no. 2 is: "Values are learned more powerfully in family interaction than any other learning situation."

FIVE

ATTITUDES SEND MESSAGES

"Life is a journey, not a destination."

MONEY AND ITS MESSAGES

We bought a new car, different from the ones we had traditionally purchased. As soon as we began driving the new car, we were aware of others like it. We had not noticed those models until we owned one. In some ways, writing a book about family and money is like that.

When I began this book I found myself listening with a new awareness to the comments I heard about money from counselees. As I was reflecting and integrating those experiences, I began to see some different "types" of attitudes emerge. When comments about money were analyzed, four "types" of money messages could be recognized.

The first is the message of *resentment.*

How difficult it is to extract money from this type. His bitter feelings expressed about money reveal his personal identification with his financial resources. To take money from him is to reduce his personal value. He builds self-worth through money. He sees demands for money as demands for a "pound of flesh." He feels personally depleted when he pays for a service. He is less resentful about the purchase of tangibles than intangibles.

Howard was one of those people. My secretary heard the message first. "Nobody is worth that much an hour," he said, when she quoted my counseling fee. He still made an appointment. When he and his wife came to see me, he made some more comments about the fee. He then proceeded to blame his wife for the way she spent "his" money. It seemed to be his philosophy that everybody wanted something from him and so he needed to defend himself against external attacks on his personal resources.

WHEN IN DOUBT, BLAME!

One of the ways Howard revealed his resentment was to blame others. As we talked together I discovered that he felt like a failure before his wife and children because he did not make more money. He resented feeling inadequate, but he measured his adequacy by the amount of his salary. To compensate, he expressed resentment toward anyone who took some of *his* money.

Blaming behavior often reflects inadequate feelings. I tried to discover the reason for Howard's sense of inadequacy. He was a perfectionist, but he could not live up to his own high standards. As a youngster, he had experienced disapproval in subtle ways. When he brought home his report card, he was not applauded for his good grades but only admonished for the poor marks. As he grew older, he felt he could never please his parents. Soon he quit trying, at least on the surface. But underneath, he still wanted their approval. Failing to get that approval, he felt hurt and rejected. His defense against these feelings of inadequacy was criticism and the rejection of others.

Another resentful “blamer” can be the pampered child. He has little maturity and resents being asked to sacrifice his own wishes in any relationship. He compensates for his sense of frustration by blaming others for any errors or inequities. He is critical of others, rejecting their attempts to relate to him. His basic feeling may be expressed in the now familiar phrase, "I'm OK-You're not OK.”

Howard is trying to retrain himself and to teach new behavior to his own children. It is very discouraging for him because of the strength of his old habits. But he now succeeds by using money as a resource for better living instead of a measure of his own worth.

BEFRIENDING YOUR BLAMER

Resentment breeds loneliness. As a person senses his isolation, he becomes even more critical of the people around him. He reinforces the trap of his own loneliness. Living with a blamer can be exasperating. It is easier to respond to his criticism by pointing out his weaknesses. His attacks heighten your defenses and feed the flame of your desire to “put him down.”

A helpful guideline for dealing with a blamer is to remember that his critical behavior tells more about him than about you. Listen to what he is telling you about his frustration and you will discover that you do not need to defend yourself, as you may have thought. His attacks then may sound humorous, even ludicrous.

Fighting with a blamer by arguing, physical confrontations, or even passive resistance only challenges him to try harder to defeat you. A resentful person needs your thoughtful reflection, your strength in resisting his intimidation, and your willingness to accept his weaknesses as well as his strengths. He may even discover in your acceptance of him the freedom to change.

WHEN YOU CAN'T WIN, QUIT!

Martha had a different problem. She appeared not to care about herself or her money. Her money signal was one of resignation. Her attitudes seemed to say, "Take it; I'm helpless. "

The first time I met Martha she reminded me of a tourist I had seen overseas. Tired and discouraged by the struggle of coping with a culture different than his own, he simply pulled from his pocket all the currency he had. In exasperation he said to the agent who spoke a different language, "Take what it costs and let me get out of here." How vulnerable.

While some find great power in money, others seem to discover only burdens and problems. Martha made enough money to manage nicely but she had no desire to take charge of her financial affairs. She never quite said the words, but her unspoken plea for therapy was "I'll pay what you ask, just take care of me." Her unwillingness to use money - *to possess her wealth* - was also a message of rejection. In this case it was self-rejection. I felt sorry for her and that was exactly what Martha wanted. She had used that methodology hundreds of times before. It began with her father. She told me about him.

"Don't worry your little head about money, darling, Daddy will take care of you." I imagined a Kentucky colonel in full confederate uniform as her description of his chauvinism poured out in the conversation. Martha's father loved her! He intended to give her security. However, he had taught her to be a helpless, resigned person. He assumed she would marry a man who would take care of her as he had done. Or perhaps she would stay at home so that he could "manage" her monetary affairs. When she moved to Atlanta in a step of independence, she learned that she was not prepared to handle money responsibly.

The first step for Martha in therapy was to pay for her own treatment. When I refused to bill her father, he became very angry with me. Several years later Martha thanked me for helping her to take the first positive step toward a new self-identity and personal management. That step initiated a sense of responsibility which began to change her life. It has not been easy for her to change, but time and effort have given birth to a new Martha. She no longer sends resignation messages about money.

Instead, she assumes full responsibility for her financial decisions and gains increased pleasure and security. What her father wanted to give her but couldn't, Martha could gain for herself and did. Overprotective parents rob their children of an individual's most rewarding asset - the right to be responsible!

LIVING WITH YOUR QUITTER

You may be married to a quitter - male or female. If you see yourself in that circumstance, here are some guidelines for self-protection, assertiveness, and loving support.

First, don't succumb to the temptation to become "Martha's father" (or his mother). Simply supporting destructive behavior in a spouse or a child is not loving. *It is cowardly.* Refuse to rescue your quitter by doing the job for her or by being seduced into "saving her from embarrassment." That behavior on your part only reinforces her weakness.

Second, give her room to grow-that includes the right to fail as well as to succeed. If she can fail and face it, she will have grasped the opportunity to succeed and live with it. *Quitters are as afraid of success as they are of failure.* Achievements bring new responsibilities and privileges. They also require new diligence. Quitting is "playing it safe." Take away the luxury of hiding in safety. Give her the chance to feel pain or pleasure for herself.

WHEN YOU ARE AFRAID, CONTROL!

Can anything improve on logic in the use of money?

When Richard and I talked about it, his arguments were so reasonable I could not disagree with him. But he came into therapy because he felt he was cold and unfeeling. In fact, in my mind I nicknamed him "the computer." I could sense his mind whir through the possible responses that he might make to a question, carefully choosing one before responding. He illustrates the third category for hidden money attitudes - rigidity!

The more I listened to "Rigid Richard", the more he reminded me of the Broadway tune, "You Gotta Have Heart." He had a rational, reasonable style; the problem was that he was locked into logical rules about money. He specifically budgeted everything he spent. He was unable to be spontaneous.

As we examined his behavior, he began to see that his exacting and careful planning had restrictions too. Feelings were missing from his system.

“No-fault” was the method but “no-feeling” was the result. Richard could risk little to chance and removed unpredictability from his life as much as possible. He had learned the rules for money management superbly. He had learned rules for living. But he had no sense of the “why” of his rules, and so he was caught in a cold, lifeless cage.

When Richard spoke to his child about doing something and was questioned, the response was, “Because it's that way.” Sometimes he said, “Because it is right to do it this way. His child was learning from the same script by which he had been taught.

The rigid life-style arises out of his past-fulfilling “parental” injunctions, laws, and demands. His robot-like life proceeds but he is a “hollow man.” Richard's military career was highly successful, but his marriage was a failure. His wife complained that she could never *feel* anything from him.

RELEASING YOUR ROBOT

Control can be a good thing, but rigidity is lifeless.

Richard was proper to a fault. He was bright, good and conservative, but almost dead!

Can you see yourself, your spouse or a child in this example? It is not too late for a change. I suggested to Richard the following steps for release from rigidity:

First, *accept the risk of being real, not perfect.*

Rigidity is a self-protective defense against personal

interaction with others. I risk no mistake or failure by controlling the people and things around me. But I miss the pleasure of sensing, touching, feeling, and loving others. Living is dangerous - it can require a reaction to a real human person rather than only a circumstance or a situation.

Second, *the anxiety of being alive is not all negative.*

Soren Kirkegaard defined anxiety as “the alarming possibility of being able.” To live is to risk! Rigidity removes the risk, but also subtracts spontaneity and joy from life. Controlling guarantees predictable results but allows little pain or pleasure.

Third, *rigid control - subjugating all feelings to unbending rules - robs life of the emotional fullness available.*

In the Broadway musical, “Mame,” there is a haunting line humorously delivered by Mame and then repeated by young Patrick which reflects his “Auntie Mame's” personal philosophy about living. She says, “Life’s a banquet, and most of us are starving! Open a new window.”

Rules can provide us with space in which to enjoy our freedom, but a rigid bondage to them can rob us of all pleasure. In dealing with an object like money, remember it is to be mastered, not to rule and master you.

FRANK IS FOURTH

A fourth money message I've discovered is *rebellion.*

Frank is a vivid example. His wife surprised me when she said, “He just refuses to pay bills.” She was tired of the confrontations with bill collectors and the phone calls she took because of late payments. So she decided to leave him. That was the crisis that forced them into counseling. They had only been married six months. As Lucile told me the story, I could understand coming home from the honeymoon and adjusting to married life must have been quite a shock. They had an expensive, memorable and very satisfying relationship while in the islands, but what she discovered about his money habits made her wonder if that had been paradise lost!

"He throws bills in the trash without ever opening them," she said. Her frustration showed in the tears that streaked down her face. "Why does he do that? Why?"

The questions asked of psychologists often perplex us as much as they do our counselees. I didn't have an immediate answer. In the appointments that followed I tried to probe Frank's rebelliousness. What I learned was surprising but understandable. His father had been a hard-working, God fearing patriot, as Frank described him. "He believed in God, his country and his union. I don't believe in any of those."

Frank's attitude was a subtle reflection of a period of time in our country's history. College students were on the rampage on our campuses. Our nation was bogged down in what appeared to be a useless war in South Vietnam. Like many others Frank felt little permanence and seemed to live only for "today." He was "anti-establishment," Lucille brought a different background and they butted heads over the use of money.

The first step for them was a compromise in procedures. Because she had to "take the heat" when a collector called about the unpaid bills, they negotiated a new system in which she would pay most of them. Frank "gave up" his authority over the process but in exchange he "gained" the privilege of having Lucile do the detail work. She took on the responsibility of bill paying, but shed most of the problems of nasty bill collectors.

Frank was not the first "money rebel" I had met, though he was probably the most difficult to analyze. He worked hard, but primarily because he enjoyed being in business for himself. What he wanted was a "hassle-free" life. As a result, he rebelled against the idea of requirements and commitments. I tried to help him to see that freedom results from fulfilling responsibilities. I'm not sure he ever did.

Unlike "Rigid Richard," Frank fought controls. His behavior bordered on the sociopathic. Many "rebels" psychologically are seeking attention. Others simply want to discover the limits of their rebellion.

Frank grew up with a father who rarely spoke to him except in correction. His mother loved him but tried to protect him from his father's punishments. His first marriage had been to a woman whose social background was very different than his own. She was a "scrapper" who grew up in the ghetto of a large city. From her, Frank learned to feel that no one cares about you but yourself. His first wife bitterly disappointed him by forsaking their marriage to run away with another man. I could understand some of his frustrations.

FREEING YOUR REBEL

Frank left counseling before any significant improvement took place. While he and Lucile worked out a new balance that temporarily helped them in their marriage crisis, Frank is probably still sending rebellious money messages to people around him. There are no simplistic solutions to all human problems. However, he reminded me that change happens only for two basic reasons: *pain or pleasure.* I will do something about my behavior only when it hurts me enough to change it, or when the reward of leaving my comfortable and secure life space seems great enough for me to risk that security to achieve it.

If you live with a money rebel, negotiate with him and fulfill your bargain. Do not take away his areas of shared responsibility. When it hurts enough or when the reward seems great enough, he'll change.

While you consider the examples I have cited, ask yourself about your own "money messages." What are you communicating to those around you through your attitudes about money? Resentment? Resignation? Rigidity? Rebellion? It may be any of these or something else. What message would you like to have your money give about you? That message will be spoken through the style incorporated in your philosophy of life as it is expressed through your use of money.

Stop for a moment and analyze your own feelings. Do people hesitate to ask you for money - perhaps because they are aware that you will "come down" on them in a blaming way? Are you an "easy mark" because of your resignation about controlling your money? Are you so rigid that there is little if any pleasure in your use of funds? Or have you simply set up for yourself an "eat, drink and be merry; for tomorrow we may die" rebellious philosophy about money?

These are the kinds of questions that lead us to take a more comprehensive and thorough look at our past. That consideration will also lead to further insight about getting more family out of your dollar.

SIX

MONEY MANAGEMENT MIRRORS

"OH, WOULD SOME POWER THE GIFT GIVE US TO SEE OURSELVES AS OTHERS SEE US.'' Robert Burns 1786

One of the things I do in counseling is reflection – that is, reporting back to the person what I have heard. This "playback" can be filled with empathy, support, intimidation, interpretation, or other feelings. The significant point is that the therapist helps build a mirror through which the counselee can see himself more clearly. The process is the same with money management. What one sees about himself as his counselor gives him an instant replay or interpretation of his past attitudes may help him to see and understand those things which he wishes to change.

In the nearly 6,000 cases I have seen, some patterns have clearly emerged about money that may serve as a mirror for you. Let me illustrate with some individuals and couples I have known. You'll recognize these people in yourself and your friends as you see them here. Enjoy them but find yourself. Then apply the appropriate principles for change in your life.

DESPERATE DIANE

Meet Desperate Diane-the girl who never has enough. Perhaps I should have called her Poor Paula. Either name would be appropriate. Her conversation is sprinkled with "I can't afford this, but ... " or "I just can't seem to make ends meet-what can I do?" Diane suffers from indecision in the use of money, therefore she always faces pressure. Choices are made poorly in the absence of careful advance planning. Her story would be humorous if it weren't so pathetic.

Her shy manipulations toward therapists or parent figures lead me to believe that her money management problems fall back into her childhood experiences. "Desperate" is indecisive, hoping someone will make a choice for her and tell her what to do. I must have heard the statement 50 times, "Someone should teach a practical course like this in high school." She sees her problem, but has little desire to discipline herself to do something about it. Reflection in counseling helped Diane to recognize her unwillingness to make decisions. She further faced an evaluation of her assets and liabilities so that she could plan an attack for change. Then she began to work out her plan. Success in the rearrangement of attitudes came slowly but it did come.

DEVEOPING DISCIPLINE

Some months later I mentally renamed her Disciplined Diane. She seemed more calm and had developed patience in sizing up priorities and then making her own choice. One day she said, “You know I am much happier now. One of the main reasons is that I feel much more in control of what I can do with myself and my resources, especially my money. Gaining control has given me more self-confidence.”

Desperation in Diane had turned into rewarding discipline. She got more out of her dollar and her relationships because of the change.

BULLISH BEN

He was as close to being a “money-holic” as I have ever known. His only goal in life seemed to be making money. He was on his way to his first million - sure that there would be a second also.

Ben lived to make money. His conversation was literally sprinkled with terms like assets, liabilities, net worth, profit margin, etc. “Money is power,” he told me. I knew he had a point. Atlanta is a financial center for the Southeast. Money speaks in this city-it has spoken for Ben. He has pursued the belief that money is the most important commodity in the universe and his behavior is consistent with his belief. He was well into the first hour we had together when I said, “Ben, if money is so powerful, buy a solution to your problem!”

It was a harsh remark, but it forced us to become honest with each other. His problem was not something but someone he couldn't buy. When he later introduced me to her, I understood more of his frustration. Julia was quite a girl! Some women would have been satisfied to have money, but she wasn't. Her refusal to accept Ben's proposal for marriage brought him up short. He was not accustomed to being told no.

RICH AND YOUNG

Ben reminded me of a New Testament story about the rich young ruler. He was described as knowing the commandments and "lacking only one thing." Jesus instructed him to sell what he had and give it to the poor. The story ended on a sad note because the young man felt the requirement was too great, and went away. Ben's story also ended on a sad point. Julia refused to marry him. She felt money was so important to him that he would never be free to love her or to love their potential children.

I thought that loss would bring Ben to his knees, but it wasn't long before new monetary quests had summoned his energies and Julia faded from his attention. She had been right. The love of making money so consumed him that he probably will never allow any person a prominent place in his affections.

As I noted Ben's case, I also changed his nickname. I now call him "Blinded Ben." There was a sense in which he never saw any color but gold. The deaths of two of the world's richest men - J. Paul Getty and Howard Hughes - occurred during the time I saw Ben. He often felt depressed and lonely, but rarely failed to reassert his basic belief in the power of money. Even when we discussed the loneliness and the reclusiveness of both of the multi-billionaires who died, he tenaciously held to his compulsive drive to make more money. At the "bottom line" he could purchase everything but a person with whom to share his wealth.

Ben may yet learn that it is not the amount of money a man has nor his net worth that deeply satisfies, but he is still "buying the best" and making the most that he can today.

MATERNAL MILDRED

That brings me to Maternal Mildred. Millie is still "earning" her way in life by sacrificing. Her conversation reflects it. She spends money on her children and her husband but cannot release her personal restrictions. She wants the best for her girls and feels badly if they need something that she can't buy. Millie's husband makes a good salary and they have few financial worries. But Millie is unhappy. She feels badly when she spends money on herself.

Millie is reacting to her childhood. When she grew up, she saw her mother as a selfish and immature person. As Millie looked back on her early years, she not only remembered her father's weakness and complaints about her mother's spending habits but she also remembered things that were missing in her life. She did not go to some school events because mother said, "We can't afford it." But Millie also remembered her mother having new clothes and things she wanted to buy even when there was not enough money to support school activities and camps that Millie wanted to attend.

So as Millie grew older, she determined she would be different. Now she made sure her girls got what they needed even if she had to do without. Millie's biggest problem was - as she saw it - a husband who just didn't care enough about the children. He spent money on himself for sports and hobbies and would buy her expensive gifts. She almost always returned the gifts and took the money to buy things "for the children." Ted became furious with her behavior and felt a distance developing between them. Eventually he had an affair with a woman where he worked and this led to their coming into counseling.

When we got beyond the stage where all Millie could do was blame Ted for his “other woman” she began to learn something about her own behavior. Eventually she recognized that her refusal to accept a gift from Ted “cut” him as surely as if she had used a razor to slash his wrists. Then she learned that her own “giving” to her children was partially a rejection of her mother's behavior rather than just an expression of her own concern. Her only happiness came in providing for them. When Millie and Ted agreed to work on their relationship, I set up some exercises for them to do in which Millie attempted to learn to receive. As she learned the joy of receiving as well as giving, she saw that Ted was pleased with giving to her. Her own attitudes changed, and she felt less guilty about spending money for herself as well as for Ted and the girls.

DEVELOPING MATURITY

Near the end of their counseling, she said, “I considered it bad to spend money for myself. It was selfish. I see now that my inhibited attitude robbed me of many of the happy experiences of doing for others. At least, much of that is passed. I'm enjoying spending money now - for my family and for me.” I can still remember the smile on Millie's face when she spoke those words.

Millie learned that what we purchase can be pleasure or pain depending on our attitudes. She learned to get more “family” out of her dollar by discarding one of the limits of the past. More self-understanding brought greater pleasure in the use of money. It was easy now to change Maternal Millie to Matured Millie as I thought about her money mirror.

LONESOME LAWRENCE

"How do you break into Atlanta's social set?" he asked me. In our first interview, I learned a lot about the man I call Lonesome Larry. "Who is keeping you out?" I queried. Then Larry began to tell me more about his frustrations. He had enough money but not a lot. He was a salaried government worker. He lived in the "right" apartment in the "right" complex. He wore the "right" clothes and made the "right" contacts. He had invited several of the single men and women of his complex to his apartment for a party. He went to great length to plan the party, getting help and advice on the hors d'oeuvres, the drinks to be served, the decorations, etc. He worked so hard and spent so much money that he was disappointed when he didn't get the kind of results he had hoped for from his friends. Some of those he invited came, but he had not been invited to their parties in the ensuing weeks. As I listened, I saw there was a certain lifelessness about Larry. He did the appropriate thing but only because he seemed to have been told that he must do those things. He mistakenly thought that most people accepted him for his monetary assets or for his propriety. Because of that he felt rejected when he was not successful in gaining recognition and friendships. Over several weeks he began to discover his sense of worth through some group experiences, particularly in a personal growth weekend where casual structuring and dress focused highly on his ability to relate emotionally, not in an expected and rehearsed manner.

Most of Larry's learning about money could be described as "snobbish." He was procedurally correct in most of his decisions but he was described by many people around him as a "calculator." He did the "right" things and he had the "right" responses to questions that were asked him, but he was dependent upon his propriety to make him acceptable.

Larry had never really been able to be a child. He had worked and done all the things that were expected of him in order to gain his parents' approval and the approval of many other adults in his world. As he grew to a greater self-understanding, one of the things that I enjoyed about Larry was that his “child” - that part of his personality that enjoyed playful and spontaneous reaction - continued to grow and develop. It was not easy for him. There were many stereotypes about proper reaction that he had to give up. One was his need to be absolutely certain that he spent “every penny” of his money logically and with reason. Larry just needed to learn to have some fun with his resources. It took several weeks of homework assignments before Larry could report some success in enjoying a spontaneous expenditure and being pleased later that he had done so.

FINDING LIKEABLENESS

In time, Lonesome Larry began to see a change in himself. His personality restrictions which expressed themselves in limited and inhibited financial patterns began to decrease. He allowed himself some new clothes and began enjoying his resources. Larry said it felt strange to him that people began to invite him to parties and for social gatherings. I invited him to explore some of these facets in a personal growth group. My role with Larry was to help him see that as he relaxed some of his restrictions, he became a more vibrant and pleasant person. When he finally concluded an the ongoing personal growth group, one of the members commented that he had finally become comfortable in calling him “Larry” instead of the more formal “Lawrence.” I agreed that Larry's new family of friends could relate to him more openly and he could enjoy himself more. Focusing on his use of money was one way of finding a new and liberating experience for Larry.

Lonesome Lawrence had been transformed into Likeable Larry.

REFLECTING

We have considered eight different behavior patterns which reveal themselves in the styles which we discussed in the earlier chapter: resentment, resignation, rigidity, and rebellion. The reflection seen in desperation, bullishness, materialism, and isolationism are further examples of the failures which cripple so many of us in the use of money. James Knight has said, "Money sickness is one of our most common illnesses but often is not recognized as such by the individual involved or by others."

More than half of the families who come for counseling have money problems. 90% of all divorces involve money conflicts and in more than 50% money is a major cause of divorce.

Our focus now shifts to three major concerns:

- assessing money philosophy
- using credit resources
- the concept of giving

PART THREE

BASIC PERSPECTIVES

SEVEN

LEARN YOUR FINANCIAL ABC'S

"TO BE WISE IS AS GOOD AS BEING RICH; IN FACT, IT IS BEITER. YOU CAN GET ANYTHING BY EITHER WISDOM OR MONEY, BUT BEING WISE HAS MANY ADVANTAGES."

Ecclesiastes 7 : 11, 12 The Living Bible

It is far too common for people to reach adulthood without having a clear, workable philosophy of money. Only when a financial crisis occurs does the problem seem to surface. Money seems to be taken for granted. However, trouble often results when we do "what comes naturally" with money.

When a couple comes to my counseling office, I usually ask them, "How do you handle money?" When I ask this question, I am hoping for insight into their philosophy and management of money. If you came into my office, how would you answer that question?

Some other important questions are: Who pays the bills? Perhaps you might ask, Who is the family treasurer? The more control vested in one person, the more resentment is likely to be present in the other members of the family. If you have a budget, how was it established? How do you modify it? Negotiations about money are strategic. They often involve much more than dollars and cents.

Bill and Jackie both seemed depressed. When I asked them, “How do you handle money?” they answered, “Poorly.” He said, “We are in such debt that we really can't afford to be here.” (Those words often give the “collector” in me cold chills!) As he explained their financial predicament, Bill obviously blamed his wife for being a careless spender. She felt hurt because she saw herself as more careful than him.

One of the most delicate and sensitive areas of interpretation I face is in helping people who think they are “right” about anything to see that they may not be. This was my problem with Bill. We began by listing the debts they had and looking at how they had decided to purchase the things for which they still owed money. When he described the purchase of the car, I got a pretty clear picture of their relationship.

They needed a new car. Bill shopped for several weeks on his lunch hour and finally decided on a rather expensive European sedan. Finally Jackie was invited to come along to choose the color and some of the equipment to be on the car. She felt the decision was made before she visited the auto dealer. She really didn't like the kind of car Bill wanted. From her conservative background, it felt pretentious. She would have preferred a less expensive car and some furniture for the house. But she had come to know Bill well enough by that time to know that he would be displeased if she refused to "help" him select the car. He was probably aware that she didn't like the car, but neither of them expressed their feelings. He was like a little boy with a new toy, but his hidden guilt at purchasing the more expensive car led to his being very willing and generous when it came to buying some expensive furniture for the house.

THE SYSTEM SURFACES

When the payments for the car, the furniture, and other items began to pinch the family's dollar, Bill bellowed about the furniture payments. At first Jackie ignored him but then countered with comments about *his* expensive car. "You liked the car too!" he said, but she felt that he was saying she was responsible for the choice of the car. Several visits later they could see their pattern. Their system called for Jackie to approve his expenditures, but in so doing obligate him to choices she wanted in other areas. He then felt guilty for manipulating her and compulsively spending. She was resentful at being blamed for the financial stress.

In working with Bill, he came to see his own insecurity as a factor which prompted him to purchase expensive items. They impressed others and made him feel more valuable. He had learned from his father "what you have shows people who you are."

Bill really loved Jackie. He felt his love was expressed in a measure by the amount of money he spent on her. This choice created a classic bind – the limits of his income and the inner need to spend. Jackie also wanted to please Bill. She had grown up in a family where money arguments seemed to contribute to more drinking by both her parents. Eventually this led to a bitter divorce in which she heard her parents call each other "irresponsible alcoholics." (That's the nicest translation I can find for a family book.) She needed to avoid conflict with Bill over money, but she deserved some things for herself. "If Bill can have an expensive car, why can't I have some nice furniture for the home? We spend more time in the home than in the car," she said bitterly. The words almost burst from her mouth between wiping the tears from her eyes and blowing her nose. It was obvious that she was struggling with some deep feelings.

Bill and Jackie are like many adults today. They are likeable, personable and basically good people. They have one major problem: neither of them has seen how their backgrounds influence their budget ideas or perhaps their non-budget ideas.

A NEW PLAN FOR AN OLD PROBLEM

My job was to help them deal first with the practical crises involving money. Before I got a banker and friend to help them consolidate the outstanding notes into a manageable loan, I carefully extracted a commitment to use some of the leftover money in their new budget for six more counseling sessions. In the next six visits we developed the ABC Plan for more family from your dollar. I hope Bill and Jackie can serve as a guide for you.

AWARENESS

First, we discovered together that *awareness* of *how* you spend, *what* you spend, and *why* you spend brings some significant insight into one's financial needs. I often refer to this process as the "in-light" time of counseling. I think I can see the lights of understanding switched on in the darkness of despair and discouragement. With Bill and

Jackie the “how” of spending under the scrutiny of our time together led not only to a better understanding of “what” was spent, i.e. a budget listing their previously fixed commitments, but the examination also revealed insight into the “why” of their spending. As Bill saw that he had tried to increase his personal psychological worth by improving his personal financial net worth, he became free to make some changes. He no longer had to “keep up with the proverbial Joneses.” He could now set a pattern which brought more satisfaction to himself and reflected his values more clearly.

BALANCE

Bill and Jackie also learned something about balancing their financial system. I assigned some homework each week when they came in. Individually they were to determine what should be included in a “must” list of expenses if their financial lives were to be satisfactory. Bill's first totaled $50 more than his take-home paycheck. It was hard for him to accuse Jackie of being the big spender after that.

We took a third sheet and built a compromise budget together. We found a place to start which would leave them not only some personal spending money but also a new savings program, modestly beginning at $10 a month.

Balance in the family dollar means understanding the income and expense picture and providing some “personal freedom” money. For Bill and Jackie, personal spending for unaccounted items began very minimally - actually at less than $25 a month for each of them. When I saw them a year later, in addition to Bill's raise, they had discovered more cost-cutting ideas and each of them had developed a personal “fund-for-fun” savings account in addition to the joint saving program they had begun earlier. The third step had already begun.

COMMITMENT

They expressed common rather than competitive goals. It was rewarding for me to hear Bill say, "Jackie really makes her dollars stretch; it is a challenge for me. I find I'm more conscious of my business expenses and have become more productive. My boss has seen the change too. The pay raise is partially the result of my feeling more at ease in my personal life. "

Jackie added that "our intimate times now seem so much better because we really enjoy being with each other. We spend more time with each other and less time *avoiding* each other by expensive entertainment.

This couple is a "showcase" of how the ABC Plan works, but there are others who have successfully managed revisions of the financial plight with the same formula.

TRY IT FOR YOURSELF

The ABC Plan involves awareness, balance, and commitment. To implement this in your family, follow these steps:

Step 1: Individually write down your expenses.

Label them "priority" - that is, the fixed and uncontrollable items including taxes, basic food costs, shelter and utility expense, minimum transportation, clothing, present installment debts, etc.

Next, determine your expenses which would be "variable"

and are perhaps the more controllable items in your budget. Some of these would fall into the next category which I often label "progress." In this "progress" category are the things I would most like to retain or add beyond the priority level in my own budget. The final category is what I sometimes label "potential." Discover who can be responsible for developing these items and begin to look at ways you can achieve them together.

"Seeing" is an amazing process. I have discovered that many of us are not seeing simply because our eyes are not open. Rufus Jones, the philosopher, once asked, "How do I know what I'm thinking until I see what I've said?"

AWARENESS

The act of writing down one's expenses and income is a test of our awareness of reality. As self-awareness is grounded in understanding, so financial awareness is founded on facts. The more you deal with the actual expenditures and costs, the less you will distort the reality of your needs and capabilities.

This simple process is capable of helping a family or individual see more clearly. As this awareness process is shared in conversations, each of the members of the family comes to understand, in appropriate measure, his part in the family's financial system.

The family that shares the most information about its resources builds a strong foundation for getting the best use of those assets.

BALANCE

Step 2: Compare your lists together.

The whole family can do this, not just the husband and wife. Balance the input from the lists and arrive at a beginning "family budget."

One family shared with me how they arrived at planning the annual vacation. They first talked about the realistic amount of money that could be allocated for that purpose. By late fall they gathered to review the past summer's trip and to plan what the next vacation could be. Over several discussions a place was chosen, the on-site costs were estimated and preparation expenses were listed. Then each member of the family set a goal his "part" in the savings program. Obviously the youngest child saved less than the other family members but all the family agreed that one result was more cooperation and less complaining when they travelled together.

In stark contrast to that is the feeling many fathers have shared with me about feeling unappreciated after spending a huge sum to "give" his family a nice trip. How sad that such an investment did not bring father and family closer together. A well planned family vacation should have a positive return emotionally.

Whether a family vacation or a priority expense is considered, when input is expected and accepted from all its members, a greater opportunity for each person to sense his importance and enjoy his participation in the money process is provided. That family grows through its dollar, not in spite of it!

COMMITMENT

Step 3: Decide together on the ways you can accomplish the changes necessary and begin together. Find some ways to show appreciation for the efforts made by each member of the family to accomplish their goals. *Share* the responsibility for achieving your goal together. Perhaps you can even create a “contest” or a “game” to record your successes.

GRIPE PIPE

I have enjoyed helping families invent tools for communication when they get together. The family “council” or meeting is a helpful and positive experience. An important ingredient is a system for handling complaints and grievances. One fun tool for this is called the” gripe pipe.”

The “gripe pipe” can be constructed of two to four cans which the ends removed and are taped together to form a long cylinder. It is used between meetings to allow members of the family to write down complaints and problems. At each meeting the pipe is opened and the contents discussed. Another family labels this meeting the “sour hour.”

Other versions of this experience included a box for each member of the family where compliments for special helpfulness can be written down and placed and then read before the whole family when it gathers.

Creativity in the process of managing money and the communication about finances can lift some of the burden and provide another key for more family sharing from your dollar.

Some special helps for doing the ABC's are shown in Part Five of this book. Be inventive and modify them for your own situation. Remember, getting more family out of your dollar may be the result of more input into the financial decision-making process by all members of the family. Initially, this process may seem daunting. Dave Ramsey so often reminds people in his financial course: “If you are willing to live like no one else, then you’ll be able to live like no one else.” More than just a play on words, this is a statement of financial peace. Initial discipline can create ultimate security and enjoyment. Only those who choose to work the program will enjoy the results!

EIGHT

POWER FOR THE PLASTIC PIT

"LET US BE HAPPY AND LIVE WITHIN OUR MEANS, EVEN IF WE HAVE TO BORROW THE MONEY TO DO IT."

Charles Farrar Brown (as Artemus Ward)

We live in a credit society and it is nearly impossible to exist without some credit accounts. Few families purchase everything they need on a "cash only" basis. Yet easy credit is a quicksand trap for many in today's world. Credit has thousands of benefits, but millions of casualties.

Some of us get into credit trouble because we have not learned how to use it. No parent does his child a favor by failing to offer some basic instruction in the credit arena. If you cannot or will not teach your child, give him a basic course in an appropriate setting. A bank or savings and loan program, a junior college, or family YMCA or YWCA program in the community can be very helpful.

CREDIT CAN CONSUME YOU

Financial consultants suggest that 20 to 25% of one's income is the maximum amount that should be committed to installment debt. Theoretically, a bank credit card can cost you nothing at all if bills are paid within the 25 day period from billing. But the credit card suppliers plan for you to use your card as an installment debt, thus creating interest charges which are profitable for them. Credit card loans, sometimes referred to as "cash advances" or "instant money" cost much more than just the interest charges and are frequently used for "emergencies." The advertising for this service often suggests that one use their credit cards in this way. There is nothing wrong with the advertising or with most bank related credit, but it can become a monster. The danger is in the fact that the more you use your credit, the easier it is for you to use it. But a day of reckoning must arrive for all of us.

SINGLES HAVE PROBLEMS TOO

Sam was single and apparently quite successful. He drove into the parking lot of our building in a new Cadillac. The suit he wore looked expensive. When he talked about his "50 grand" a year job I was aware that money was important to him. "I have never been so depressed," he told me. As we talked further he told me about his previous job before he moved to Atlanta, leaving behind a girlfriend and changing his way-of-life. In spite of the fact that he was making almost double the salary of his previous job, his unhappiness increased as he sought various ways to find pleasure. He "bought things" and "changed things" to allay the emptiness he felt. He moved into a new apartment; he bought a new car; he ate at expensive restaurants; and he took girlfriends to extravagant entertainment. Soon he had a money problem. A friend suggested that he come to see me.

"Money is not your problem, Sam," I said when we met for our evaluation session together. I'd seen him four previous visits to gather data, do psychological testing, and generally get to know him. The evaluation process gives us both something to begin working with each other. I get to know my counselee and he gets to size-up his counselor. I explained to Sam that the depression he was experiencing seemed complicated by his financial problems. He was in debt! However, the emptiness which he felt could not be "purchased away."

It is true that money can be a therapy for many of us under certain circumstances. Occasionally buying a new outfit can give us an emotional lift that is beneficial. However, repeating this process impulsively had gotten Sam into a large credit hole. He was trying to "buy" friendship and even love. He had people around him readily and he was often "rewarded" for an expensive evening by spending the night at his date's apartment. But Sam was still lonely. The more he spent, the greater the pressure and even greater was his feeling of emptiness.

For Sam the financial problem was fairly easy to handle. By some crash discipline, he was out of debt within six months, and he felt better about his money problem. During this time we also worked on his loneliness, through having him participate in a personal growth experience. Because he could not spend money on the growth group, he discovered he had "something to give" to people in relationships that was more important than money. One day, when we reviewed his progress in an individual session, he said, "It is a shame to finance your loneliness!" I agreed.

CONVENIENCE, NOT MANAGEMENT

Sam taught me some other lessons about credit. Like budgets, the ABC (awareness - balance – commitment) plan works.

Credit cards are for *convenience* but should not be used for general purchasing or money management. A good rule of thumb is that you should be able to reduce your outstanding credit card balance in no more than 60 days without disturbing the rest of your budget. If you consistently make the minimum payment required on a credit card, you are not using your credit cards well. Credit cards provide an opportunity for deferring at the moment cash is needed, bur can become unrealistic ways of managing money when one begins to accept the "deferred payment plan" which the credit card offers. The best use of Sam's credit cards came for him when he was able to charge no more than he could payoff in full on each billing. This was true for two reasons: One, Sam felt like he was really controlling his expenses, in spite of the fact that he was still charging some things. And two, he used his credit cards as a way of recording his expenses and helping him check out the budget items he had established.

Credit is probably a permanent part of our society. It would be unwise for a twentieth century man to attempt to turn back the clock. Learning to use *credit wisely* is better than trying to avoid credit.

Robert Schuller , the retired host of the "Hour of Power" tells of an incident when he was twenty-two that illustrates a good credit policy. He calls it "never borrow money for coal."

When I left Western Seminary and went to my first

pastorate in Chicago, Illinois, I lived in the church parsonage. It was heated with coal, and when October came, I needed coal for the furnace. One of the men in the church said, “Well, it'll take about five tons of coal to get you through the winter. At fifteen dollars a ton, that's seventy-five dollars.”

I didn't have seventy-five dollars so I called up the coal yard and asked, “Will you deliver five tons of coal?” “Yes.”
“Will you charge it, please?” “Oh, we don't charge coal.” “You're kidding!” “Oh, no, not at all. Guess you'll have to borrow it from the bank.” I hung up. At the bank, I asked, “Would you loan me money for coal?” “Oh, no,” the banker replied, “we don't loan money for coal. “'What he didn't say, and what he meant was, “You're only twenty-two years old and you're new at all this, so you don't know any better.” Then the banker said, “I tell you what, Rev. Schuller. I'll loan you money for coal this time, but never again.” “Why not?” I asked. “Well,” he explained. “You will burn up that coal. If you don't pay us back our seventy-five dollars, what do we get in return? Nothing! It's all gone up in smoke.”

That banker then gave me some of the soundest advice I've ever received: “Never borrow money for coal. You want to borrow money for a car, for a house, come to us. And all we will say is, 'Can you make the monthly payments?' If you've got the cash, or the salary coming in to make the monthly payments, we'll loan you money on that house or car.

Then if you can't pay the mortgage back, we take the house or the car and sell it. If there's any money left over after we get paid, you get it. We call that equity. But, he went on, never borrow money for the gasoline you put in the car.

Never borrow money for the tires you put on the car. Never borrow money for the spark plugs. Never borrow money for coal."

PITTFALLS OF CREDIT

Learning to use credit correctly is the key out of the plastic pit. Examine your family's financial picture and avoid these three pitfalls:

1. *Borrow basically* for the purchase of tangible assets. It is probably best not to borrow for luxuries, although the definition of that word is changing. Items for which you borrow should maintain some intrinsic value throughout. the life of your credit for that item.

2. *Borrow thoughtfully*. Do not borrow impulsively. Laws in most of the U.S.A. have provided a three day "cooling off' period for installment contracts. If the government seeks to protect you, accept its benefits! Better yet, think over carefully your "instinct" to borrow. Decide only after having carefully weighed the positives and the negatives. Waiting a day will usually produce favorable results.

3. *Borrow for your budget not against it!* Budgeting is not effective unless it is followed. Once you commit yourself to a plan, revise it only when you have fulfilled the original commitment or when the changes improve the handling of your money.

REFINANCING OR CONSOLIDATION

Gaining control of the course of your financial stream may not be easy. A careful and honest analysis with a trusted

[1] *Schuller, Robert H., "Your Church Has Real Possibilities!" (Regal Books: Glendale, California, 1974)*

and reputable finance person can be a good first step.

One of the techniques suggested may be a major refinancing of your indebtedness. This should result in your ability to meet your obligations on a regular basis. Refinancing is *not* a process to be used regularly for clearing out your drawers of bills resulting from more impulsive spending. Refinancing is a control measure.

After refinancing, discipline is required in order to adhere to your budget and make the plan work. If you continue to buy impulsively, it is a sign of a non-monetary need-one which should be explored with a marriage and family counselor or psychologist. More marriage and family counselors have had experiences dealing with the stresses related to money than almost any other professional group.

To find a qualified person to help you, check with a reputable professional organization.

For a marriage and family counselor, call or write:
American Association of Marriage and Family Therapy, 112 South Alfred Street, Alexandria, Virginia 22314-3601, aamft.org, (703) 838-9808

For a psychologist, contact the:
American Psychological Association, 750 First Street, Washington, D.C. 20002-4242, apa.org, (800)374-2721

For the nearest non-profit financial counseling agency, a good resource is:
National Foundation for Consumer Credit, Inc. 2000 M Street, N.W., Suite 505, Washington, D.C. 20006, (800) 388-2227

For a Christian financial program, contact Dave Ramsey's Financial Peace University, 1749 Mallory Lane, Brentwood, TN 37027 (888) 227-3223

Living in a credit pit, whether from poor use of credit cards or from impulsive borrowing, can be like struggling in quicksand - the more you move the deeper you sink. To get out of that sinking spot, you need a resource outside yourself. Don't be afraid to risk asking for help. The pain of admitting you need help will be offset by the relief of beginning on the path to new control of your finances. As financial pressure is reduced, the energies you have consumed in those struggles will be freed for other interests. Behind the mountain of unpaid bills you may find your family waiting.

NINE

KEEP WHAT YOU GIVE AWAY

"THE ONLY LOVE WE KEEP IS THE LOVE WE GIVE AWAY."

"IF YOUR PROFITS ARE IN HEAVEN, YOUR HEART WILL BE THERE TOO."
Matthew 6 : 21 The Living Bible

Much of our money concerns center on achieving the "good life." Few of us would want less for our children than we have had ourselves. We often teach all the lessons about money to our children except the most important ones.

Simply put, the most important lesson that I have ever learned about money is this: *Money turned outward is more rewarding than money turned inward.* When you read Charles Dickens' Christmas Story about the miser Scrooge, you see an illustration of this principle. Hoarding money misses the meaning of money.

Money is a medium of exchange. Most effectively money transfers resources. As inflation occurs, money's meaning and therefore its value is decreased. Recession occurs when money is withheld; then hoarding it seems important. Values are expressed in the investment of money. What I give for something expresses the sense of worth that I place in that object. This is also reflected in my general life-style as I consider the things in which I choose to invest money.

In the historic Hebrew tradition, Jesus talked a lot about money. He had a singularly unified philosophy about money, of the material and the spiritual, about the temporal and the eternal. There are no neat distinctions existing for division; there are no compartments for isolation within His teachings about money.

THREE GUIDING PRINCIPLES

To express the idea that money turned outward is more rewarding than money turned inward, I have come to use three cardinal rules for myself:

One, the *more money* I have, the *more carefully* I need to use it, both to avoid failure and to gain the maximum happiness from its potential.

Two, the more I *express people values* in the use of my money, the more overflow in *material values* I will experience from it.

Three, the *sacrificial* investment of money in the lives of others is a more lasting pleasure than investing the *surplus* in giving. Let me expand on these ideas with some real life experiences.

A SECRET OF SUCCESS

Over forty years ago I opened my private practice of marriage and family counseling. By most standards I have been successful. When I was recently asked to give an address at a professional meeting, a friend said, "what is the secret of your success?" As I thought a moment, I responded, "Perhaps most essential is keeping your priorities in mind." The more we talked, the more I realized how that idea dominates my own use of money.

The risking man can become the rich man. The more you give away the more you can keep. The first step toward that end is one of management. When I have more money, I have more responsibility, not less.

Here are some simple ideas that work for putting priorities in place financially.

YOU ARE WHAT YOU SPEND

How often have you heard someone say, "You can't take it with you?" *I believe you can!* As I manage money, the more I add or delete experiences that affect the kind of person I am. When I buy a new suit, I enjoy wearing it. I add positive feelings about myself to the inner calculator of my worth. If I buy a suit and punish myself for spending too much on it, my internal reflections from that experience are negative and inhibit my feeling of worth.

When in the conflict of my private world, I record negative judgments about myself a point for depression is made. If I evaluate my decision positively, the score is recorded on the side of expression. I feel *down* when I use my resources poorly. I feel *up* when I use them wisely.

In the use of money, depressed people feel negatively about past decisions and therefore tend to compound the process by repeating poor judgment. Happier people feel good about the past use of funds and are likely to continue to express themselves positively.

THE RICH GET RICHER

“Rich” attitudes give birth to “rich” relationships! Each of us is like a contagious disease. We infect the sphere of the life of those with whom we have contact.

During my internship at Long Beach Memorial Hospital some years ago, the chaplain taught me an important lesson. In listening to different patients' problems, you can become “loaded” with them. Some emotional garbage can be “unloaded” when you visited another patient's room. In a similar way, negative experiences may accumulate internally within us. Depending on one's personality, these experiences may drain energy and lead to depression or may result in what appears to be an “unexpected” explosive response.

That expresses the truth negatively. In the positive sense the experiences which I feel are beneficial also accumulate. An attractive and helpful overflow then occurs to persons around you. Applying that specifically to your family, self-approving financial feelings will become the base for more positive responses to other members of your family. As you learn to manage carefully, you will not only feel better within but will maximize that benefit to those around you, especially your family members.

STRUCTURE LIBERATES

I have avoided terms like “conservative” and “liberal.” Those words, when applied to money, usually reflect matters of style. What is more basic is that an understanding of one's own structure - or the absence of it - is the beginning of attitude liberation.

Having mastered the ABC Plan or some other pattern provides a structure out of which financial freedom can be expressed. A budget is like a highway. If followed, the road will bring you to a desired destination. Along the way speed limits and the rights of others on the road must also be observed. A map for the trip, like a global positioning device, may also give one confidence in his direction. Your financial plan is a responsibility, but out of that can grow a new sense of freedom. That freedom will be enhanced by your observing financial rules, respecting the rights of other members of your family and using your budget as a guideline to give you confidence.

MONEY IS NOT YOUR MASTER

When you gain control financially and exercise that control, there is a new feeling of power. But when your problems overwhelm you, a sense of frustration results. One aspect of that frustration is the feeling of being helpless.

I sensed the relief in Walter's expression when he arrived at a plan for financial management. By the time he had disciplined himself for three months, he was experiencing a growing confidence. When the first year of our work ended, he and his wife were aglow with pride at accomplishing their plan. They had used a structured money plan successfully; the result was a new sense of freedom for both of them. They were no longer slaves to their bills, but had become the managers of their resources. But real riches only begin with what you have and how you manage them.

PEOPLE HAVE PRIORITY

The second phase of keeping what you give away is in “people values.” Do you remember Fanny Brice's lyrics in the Broadway show “Funny Girl”? “People who need people are the luckiest people in the world.” I believe in that quote. Its application to material values is what concerns me here. How do I express “people values” ?

Perhaps remembering a crisis experience will be helpful here. In spite of staggering hospital costs, few of us weigh those costs against the value of the person's life. The usual response is the desire to save the life and then worry about paying the bills. If that principle can be extracted and applied to the non-crisis experiences, another key to satisfaction will be identified.

THINK HUMAN

In my office a wall poster says: “Caution: Human Beings Here, Handle with Care.” I bought the poster recently, but the concept has been a possession of my mind for some years. Like poetry I'm glad for posters, songs, quotes, and other expressions of human value that express what I feel. Writing for me is a discipline for sharing values. When I read a book, I am affirmed by those things that succinctly state my feelings. I am also helped by those statements that challenge my assumptions. Often I am benefited most by those thoughts which seem different from my own. Your ideas about what it means to think human may be different from mine, but let me share with you my “human beings handled here” guideposts. I call them:

FIVE AFFIRMATIONS OF PRICELESS PERSONHOOD

1. I want to see beyond appearances, to know real “worth” in as many people as I can.

2. I promise myself to use money to enhance my relationship with others, not to try to create “value” in myself or others.

3. I do not believe people are “for sale,” I will not try to “buy” another human being, I may do a service for a fee, but my integrity is beyond the reach of money.

4. I will use money to support better human interaction not to interfere with it.

5. I owe no one more than consideration, justice and an honest exchange of ourselves.

When I practice these affirmations I experience not only better feelings but more actual money through which to share who I am with others.

GIVING BUT KEEPING

It may seem contradictory to you to think in these paradoxical terms. You can only keep what you give away. If you can grasp this balance, you can get the most from life. Not all of us are alike. Some folks seem comfortable with things the way they appear. I am an insistent seeker of truth and feel challenged by discovery. My personal pilgrimage through life has been in many ways an attempt to synthesize the truth I have discovered in psychology, sociology, theology, and other disciplines of thought. Getting more family out of your dollar is a specific part of a larger quest in all of us: *getting the most out of life!*

How I use money in relation to people is a place where truth is tested by practice. It is not what I say but what I do that reveals my character.

REALISTIC REFINING

Two beliefs are important to the discovery of the joy of giving: *one*, you can only *possess* what you are not afraid to lose and *two*, giving away what you have makes you part of all you *share.*

I have experienced the possession-loss statement with so many people in counseling. When husbands and wives argue over money, the issue is power. From sharing those conflicts, I realized that only the husband who is not afraid of losing his wife can really "have and hold" her.

A good marriage is two people who can say, "I don't *have* to live with you, but I *want* to be here." With money, the more I grasp it to myself, the more I am aware of my inability to hold it. I can only enjoy it when I am unwilling to be possessed by it. I can then lose it and not be personally diminished.

In 1955 on the day Jim Elliot died in a jungle in South America, he wrote these profound words in his diary: "He is no fool who gives what he cannot keep to gain what he cannot lose."

PRACTICAL PERSPECTIVE

I want to share with you a practical and personal experience of handling money. With virtually no money, I opened a professional office. However, I believed that what you give away is what you keep. From the first month it became a practice to set aside a certain percentage of the gross receipts to use for charitable purposes. I began with ten percent as a guiding figure. Over the years that figure increased dramatically, not only in the total amount of money but in the percentage set aside. The reason is the ***joy*** I receive from giving money away. The days I feel like the richest man in town are the days of the month I have the opportunity of sharing those resources with causes around the world. In a sense I can become a part of a child in Korea or Indonesia, a hospital in South America, or a family's need in Africa.

The example is monetary, but the truth is psychological and spiritual. As you extend yourself through giving, you gain priceless treasures that can never be taken away. Recession does not diminish their value. You cannot lose them in a depression.

The *joy* of the gift is the reward you will keep forever. Giving frees you to receive what others give you. Reaching out to another gets you close enough for him to touch you.

MY MONEY PRAYER

Lord, I am tempted by money. Its apparent power seduces me. Keep me from being willing to measure my inner worth against the amount of money I possess. Help me not to measure another man's value by that standard.

I am tempted to see money as an answer to problems. I think, "If I only had ..." and follow that thought with a financial quote. I do not really believe that life is measured in the abundance of things or the lack of them; yet I am tempted. Keep me from spending money as a means of relating to people. Help me to see clearly the pitfalls as well as the joys in the use of money.

I have learned that "giving" brings happiness. I can translate some of me into money and thus share with my world. Thank you for that insight. Help me, however, not to substitute "buying something" or giving a check instead of really giving myself. I believe that where my treasure is, my heart - the sense of life involvement and impulse - will be too. Help me to see how best to use all the resources I have.

I want my money to express the highest and the best in me. But so often it is like a fire. When properly used, it may warm me and cook my food. If improperly controlled, it may destroy my shelter and even my body. I need the proper control over money. I want to learn how to warm my world in the way I use money and not consume myself. Help! For the sake of one who gave his all for me, I pray. Amen.

Personal perspectives have special application to the family in the areas of conflict, training, and developing intimacy. The basic approaches we have considered in part three lead us now to look at some positive directions that you can take to get more family out of your dollar.

PART FOUR

POSITIVE DIRECTIONS

HOME IS WHERE YOU CAN BE SILENT AND STILL BE HEARD ...

WHERE YOU CAN ASK AND FIND OUT WHO YOU ARE ...

WHERE PEOPLE LAUGH WITH YOU ABOUT YOURSELF ...

WHERE SORROW IS DIVIDED AND JOY MULTIPLIED ...

WHERE WE SHARE AND LOVE AND GROW...

TEN

HANDLING FAMILY MONEY CONFLICTS

"MONEY MAY BE THE HUSK OF MANY THINGS, BUT NOT THE KERNEL. IT BRINGS YOU FOOD, BUT NOT APPETITE; MEDICINE, BUT NOT HEALTH; ACQUAINTANCES, BUT NOT FRIENDS; SERVANTS, BUT NOT LOYALTY; DAYS OF JOY, BUT NOT PEACE OR HAPPINESS ..."

Most families argue about money. Research percentages vary from approximately 55 % to 65 %, but a majority of us at one time or another have arguments about finances.

The issues are usually about who spends what and how they spend it. Disagreements occur in wealthy families and poor ones. Some fight over not having enough while others fight about who spends the most without consideration for other members of the family.

POWER STRUGGLES

Please recognize two essential problems in money disagreements. First, they aren't usually about money and second, the struggle is compounded by a process of poor communication. It has been my experience that more than 80% of the family fights that center around money are power struggles in disguise. They boil down to the raw question: Who's in charge here?

The two most commonly used weapons in marital conflict are money and sex. There was a time when men controlled the money and women controlled sex. That often meant a "barter" system was established- "quid pro quo" - in which each gave something to get something in return. When the children get into the argument, they often include other power sources, such as the opinions of their peers to put added pressure on parents. Grandparents and other relatives can also be drawn into the conflict or can voluntarily participate depending on the amount of power investment they see in the situation. Each party to the conflict wants some power to maintain his position. However, most families camouflage the struggle.

Mix the hidden power struggle with the barriers to communications and the results are often explosive. Dad isn't so upset about the ten dollar item charged at the department store, but he bellows about that particular thing as a way of expressing his feeling about not being appreciated as the family bread winner. Mom and teenagers usually "blow-up" over insignificant things when more important issues lie behind their reactions.

BASIC ASSUMPTIONS

If your family is experiencing money conflicts, do not – I

repeat – DO NOT try to *stop* having conflict! You will fail miserably. Conflict is a natural part of life. You cannot avoid conflict; what you can do is to learn to handle it constructively. My assumption is that the families who attempt to avoid conflict destroy themselves. The families who learn to manage conflict also learn to grow in other ways and build stronger relationships with each other.

Another basic assumption is that learning to manage family conflicts is a process *not* a miracle. You will all learn together and probably slowly. Just wanting to minimize the conflicts helps and reading this book may offer some suggestions, but a regular and consistent effort will be the key to change.

GOOD GUIDELINES

Here are some guidelines to start the process of conflict management. Think of them as you might a rope. The rope is to be used to bring in your horse which is free in the pasture. Having the rope won't guarantee you can catch the horse, but it can certainly help. If you catch the horse, it will be a lot easier to get him back to the barn. These guidelines will have to be practiced by the family to make them succeed; but if you bring some destructive forces under control, there will be a lot of energy left which you can use for more positive things.

FACE IT FRESHLY

Conflict management begins when a situation arises. Handle it as soon as possible. Face it freshly! You may not be able to completely settle the issue, but you can acknowledge the differences of opinions and set a time to discuss it further.

Disagreements are like food. Leftovers become stale. As the spoiling process increases, so does the distastefulness. What was once palatable has become garbage. When some families argue it looks like a garbage fight. Everyone has his own supply of leftover grievances.

"Stuffing back" your feelings or "gunny-sacking" them only increases your chances for dumping the whole load on the wrong person. It also raises the possibility of your being angry and upset about something for several days or weeks when the other person is not even aware of your feelings.

"TENSE" TALKS

As practically as possible, face your problems in the present tense. It is much easier to say "I feel now" than to try to remember what you felt yesterday. The "now" argument or discussion also tends to be less distorted from reality.

"It is easier to keep quiet until a conflict passes," Helen said, when she described her family problems. Her husband travelled and she just waited for him to leave home. What developed for them was a refrigerated atmosphere - lots of cold shoulders!

In typing class a line for practice was "now is the time for all good men to come to the aid of their country." I practiced that typing until I memorized the keys. I want to apply it to families in conflict. *Now is the time for honest members to handle family problems.*

Teach your children (or your parents) that now means "no old waiting." It could also mean "no old waste." Withholding your feelings is unfair to your family and destructive to yourself. Specialists in internal medicine agree that unresolved tensions contribute significantly to heart problems, ulcers, and intestinal stress along with other physical symptoms. These are often the result of storing up one's feelings inside and failing to release them. This increases the tension level within one's body. Now is the time to share your feelings with members of your family-*not tomorrow*-today. The first guideline you must master is to face conflict freshly.

COURTESY CULTIVATES

Without being phony, you can deal with conflict courteously. Rudeness is not a virtue. Nor is volume or violence. The truth can be spoken in love more effectively because it will be heard. Few of us would walk away from a friend or a neighbor who was speaking to us. Yet, among the most common complaint of spouses about dirty fighting tactics is that of “walking away.” Some can manage to close out the world and not hear a thing. Withdrawal is a passive but unfair defense. Whether you leave the room or simply internally withdraw into yourself, you have withdrawn and summarily dismissed the person with whom you are in conflict.

Let me suggest some other ways to courteously deal with conflict. When a member of your family yells at you, lower your voice when you speak. Soon he too will lower his voice. He will not be able to hear what you say if he doesn't. Your calmness, even if only reflected in the quietness of your voice, will also be a reminder to him of how foolish he sounds screaming at the top of his lungs. One of the most discourteous and unfair ways of increasing conflict is to ignore someone in the family who speaks to you. Teenagers often perfect the shoulder shrug. Dads behind newspapers ignore with the “uh-huh” grunts which are no real assurance of communication from without or from within. Courtesy in the conflict situation demands attention to what is being said. Unspoken expressions of hostility are also discourteous. One of the difficulties of a slammed door, a banged drawer or even a quiet tear is that it may require mind reading to be interpreted. Few of us have such psychic powers. Play it safe in your family. Be understood. There is nothing in the nature of conflict that deletes courtesy. Master this second principle "confront courteously."

ONE AT A TIME

Some years ago a boxer fought three men in the same contest and beat them all, but he fought them one at a time. The third guideline for productive handling of conflict is like that fighter's tactic: stick to the issue!

A common tactic when parents and teenagers argue is for the parent to change the subject-particularly if he feels that he is losing ground in the contest. "And another thing I have been wanting to say to you" is usually an indicator that your ground is shaky. Discipline yourself to stay on the subject of disagreement. A second issue can be introduced only when the first one is settled. Trying to divert the conflict to another issue is a distracting tactic and usually fails to settle either the first issue or the second one.

Of course, it is appropriate for a family to discuss an agenda of things to be decided and to postpone some of the issues registered, by mutual consent, when time runs out.

Susie was one of the brightest twelve year olds I had ever met. She was also very frustrating. Although her family wanted her present in our sessions, she was not "part of our problem" according to her parents' introduction to me. An older son was the "identified patient" in the family. When they came to me I suggested the whole family come in for the session so that I could get a clear picture. I soon saw Susie was the family "distracter."

As I worked with the family, I learned that Susie was modeling the behavior of her mother away from my office. It was nearly impossible to settle an issue because either mom or daughter would attempt to change the focus. It was no wonder that the family picture was blurred. When a camera is out of focus, the result is a poor picture. This family had a picture of each other and of themselves that was hazy and indistinct because of distracting behavior.

Only a tape recorder played back to Susie and her family turned the corner in the family sessions. The conflict was handled when all the family members began to practice the third guideline: stick to the issue.

PLAY IT BY EAR

The fourth guideline is one of the secrets of good communication: listen as much as you talk. In order to manage conflict you need to understand the other person's point of view as well as stating your own. Listening helps you to understand what the other person IS saying.

Clarification is an important tool. Have your family practice in peacetime so that you can clarify in the heat of battle. Here are some good responses to check up on your listening skills. Try them on each other. Did I understand you to say? If I heard you correctly, you said... I want to understand you. Please repeat. Could I repeat what you said to me to make sure I understood?

One of the problems for many families in handling conflict is eye training. We are so accustomed to the battle that we simply watch the mouth and think about what we will say as soon as it stops moving. What we need is more ear training-help in the basic ability to listen. It is so important for each of us to be heard.

Some people are so lonely and anxious to be heard, that they are willing to pay a hundred dollars per hour to know that a therapist is listening to what they say. One author has even described psychotherapy as the "purchase of friendship." It is sad but amusing to observe what happens when we don't listen. Let me illustrate:

A MISSED COMMUNICATION

"Mary is so stubborn," Joe began. I was uncertain where he was going with his beginning, but he eventually praised Mary for being stubborn enough not to give up until he could understand her position. He closed his monologue with words like "and we've made most of this progress because of her. If she hadn't dragged me in here, we might have gotten a divorce. I sure love her, Doc, and I'm glad we came."

I knew what to expect because Mary had closed her eyes when he spoke the word "stubborn." She almost threw the lamp when she said, "that makes me so mad." Realizing that she had not listened to Joe, I stopped and asked her to tell me what he had said. Joe looked amazed. Mary had heard little after "stubborn." Fortunately, the tape recorder was on and proved to her that he really did say what I repeated to her before I played it back.

Joe made a poor choice of opening lines for his commendation speech about Mary. If they had not been in the office, another battle about who said what would have occurred. Instead they both learned the importance of listening when you aren't the speaker.

In the management of conflict, listening is at least as important as speaking. You may be surprised to hear someone saying something nice about you instead of what you imagined you heard or would hear.

NEGOTIATE NATURALLY

The fifth guideline is: negotiate naturally. That simply means we are to be willing to compromise. In every family conflict the solutions that we can live with are the result of hard work at clarifying, listening, and compromising.

Families often react like the humorous statement: “My mind is made up. Don't confuse me with the facts!” Teenagers often complain that they know the answer before the question is asked- “No!” Parents should take the lead in establishing the rules for the family-democracy will not work in the home. All children need loving limits in their lives. But it is also important for parents to be ready to hand the reins of management over to their children when they are ready to responsibly regulate themselves.

When the teenager period arrives in life, the telephone is almost automatically an issue. This is particularly true with girls, although I have noticed that both my sons have also created lots. of busy signals on our line. For Father's Day, near her 15th birthday, my daughter gave me a humorous card which began, “Dad, I'll always remember those words you spoke constantly in my youth.” When I opened the card, in huge letters I read, “GET OFF THE PHONE!”

We laughed about the card, but we have argued many times about the length of calls, the time appropriate for use of the telephone, etc. One of our negotiations resulted in a second telephone which only rings in the rooms of our three children, all of whom are teenagers. Now they fight with each other about who is being fair with the telephone!

Discipline is important, but so is compromise. The road between childhood and adulthood is a tough one. Remember to give your parents all the help you can. Learn how to negotiate. Here are some guidelines to ponder:
What steps can I take to make the problem less painful?
Have I considered thoroughly the point made by my "opposition"?

What would I like to suggest to bring us closer together in our differences?

What is it that I want that would settle our present conflict? It is said that lovers' quarrels are half fight, and half the fun of making up. Families can also benefit from that prescription. Let your negotiations be the kind that can bring you back to the point of making up.

The final guideline for managing conflict is: bury the hatchet when the fight is finished. Be sure the bell has sounded to end the round and the decision has been reached. Then do your best to bring about reconciliation after a conflict has been handled, especially within the family. You can learn some healing words, even when you firmly believe in the position you have been defending. Try some of these after your next conflict:

I hurt when we disagree. I am sure you do too. I'll be glad when we have resolved this.

I enjoy our good times so much more than these conflicts. I'm glad our love is bigger than our disagreements. It is good but painful to be part of a family that cares enough to confront.

It is truly the secure person who is ready to do battle over an issue, bur never willing to let the issue stand between him and one he loves.

Your family will probably be in the minority if you take these guidelines seriously and practice them. It will require an effort, but any family can fail at handling money conflicts. I want the kind of family that can get up off the floor after a "knock-down drag-our" and fall back into each other's arms. What kind do you want?

ELEVEN

LEARNING PRACTICAL CONCEPTS TOGETHER

IF A CHILD LIVES WITH CRITICISM, HE LEARNS TO CONDEMN.
IF A CHILD LIVES WITH HOSTILITY, HE LEARNS TO FIGHT.
IF A CHILD LIVES WITH RIDICULE, HE LEARNS TO BE SHY.
IF A CHILD LIVES WITH SHAME, HE LEARNS TO FEEL GUILTY.
IF A CHILD LIVES WITH TOLERANCE, HE LEARNS TO BE PATIENT.
IF A CHILD LIVES WITH ENCOURAGEMENT, HE LEARNS CONFIDENCE.
IF A CHILD LIVES WITH PRAISE, HE LEARNS TO APPRECIATE.
IF A CHILD LIVES WITH FAIRNESS, HE LEARNS JUSTICE.
IF A CHILD LIVES WITH SECURITY, HE LEARNS TO HAVE FAITH.
IF A CHILD LIVES WITH APPROVAL, HE LEARNS TO LIKE HIMSELF.
IF A CHILD LIVES WITH ACCEPTANCE AND FRIENDSHIP, HE LEARNS TO FIND LOVE IN THE WORLD.

A psychiatrist asked a patient on one occasion: "Did the feeling of inferiority come over you suddenly, or did it develop normally with marriage and parenthood?" Another humorist has said that by the time a couple can really afford to have children, they are having grandchildren. Finally, an allowance is what you pay your children to live with you. When I thought about how this book would develop, I knew that this would be one of the more difficult chapters to write.

I wish I could offer you seven secrets to stress free stability in the family, but I can't. Before I had children, I was sure I knew about them. After I became a father my assurance was subdued. With three teenagers I humbly offer these suggestions!

We can be sure of one thing-strong families produce strong children. But your next fair question is, What is a strong family? And how can I make mine strong?

Here are five identifying characteristics of the family whose atmosphere is strong:

1. The members love each other. Loving means I like the people in my family. I express appreciation for them and to them. I want to make them feel important and worthwhile. I emotionally support them. We share together quality of care.

2. The members talk to each other. The lines of communication are open and used. Conflicts are faced and discussed. Conversations that are fun as well as serious are regular features of daily living. Questions are explored and answers found together.

3. The members belong to each other. They share themselves qualitatively and there is a bond that holds them to each other. A spiritual unity is expressed in common goals and values. They can pull together because they are moving in the same directions emotionally.

4. The members enjoy being with each other. They spend time doing family activities and often give priority to family plans over other activities. It is natural for them to share their family life with each other because they are proud to be part of this unit.

5. The members are independent of each other. Each of the

family members, at appropriate ages, can function without leaning on the family. They often do and because of the variety of their individual interest, the family group is more interesting, diverse, and complex. Each member's uniqueness is a part of the intricate balance of the unit.

If these characteristics are in your family, you are already transmitting strong signals on clearly defined frequencies to your children. Your behavior is the ultimate judge of these characteristics. The now famous lines of Dorothy Law Nolte which introduced this chapter remind us of that fact.

Let me illustrate these five facets of family strength.

Some parents are fearful their children will ask embarrassing questions. Strong families talk openly with each other. Questions provide an opportunity for sharing feelings 'and information. The kids are usually smart enough not to wait for too little, too late.

Myron and Cynthia lived on a farm and had a very relaxed view of animal reproduction and human sexuality. A very tense, unmarried school principal referred little Roger to my office because of "emotional problems." What I uncovered was Roger's very open sharing with his classmates of the way the cows, dogs, and horses delivered their babies. Roger even knew that human children weren't delivered by the stork.

Talkative, but not emotionally disturbed, Roger went back to school, but my next conference was with the principal.

Apparently some "other parents" were upset by the information their children gained from Roger's reports. I was finally invited to address the PTA on the subject. Basically what I said was never be afraid to answer questions your children ask, no matter what the subject. It is the questions they don't ask or won't answer that are dangerous.

Strong families can openly discuss any issue, sometimes seriously and often humorously, without embarrassment. Be thankful if your children talk to you and take a bow if they listen. You still have a strong parent-child relationship.

TEN TIPS ON TALKING

While thinking about talking, let me share with you some very practical pointers to improve your family conversations.

1. Say what you feel as well as what you think. Fathers especially need to be reminded that your heart says some things so much better than your head. Loving words sometimes make more “sense” than logic. Never be afraid to tell a member of your family how you feel. They probably already know and it will make them feel better to have you acknowledge what their senses are picking up.

2. Separate people and behavior whenever possible. Mother's actions may be miserable; hopefully mother isn't. Tell her you don't like what she said or did, but you still love her. That is the single most important distinction one can make in communicating with others to distinguish between what you are and what you do.

3. Speak specifically about actions. Your children don't “always” or “never” do anything. Those are accusing and humiliating terms; they hurt. Generalizing and blaming in your verbal communication will only guarantee you a defensive response from someone you love. Don't generalize; it won't help at all.

4. Be congruent. Don't speak with a “forked tongue”. Let your words and your feelings match. Satire is safe, but it is often painful. Sarcasm may get a laugh now, but the tears may fall later. When you send two signals in the same message, it is a sure sign of only one thing: you are afraid to stand on either one of them alone.

5. Leave analysis to the psychologists. Interpreting his behavior won't impress him. He could probably care less about what it means to you. Your feelings are what count-your analysis will usually be wasted, even if it is brilliant! Tell him what you heard and respond to that. He will resent your responding to what he doesn't think he said.

6. Nobody in your family can read your mind. You will have to tell them why you are upset, quiet, depressed, etc. Don't expect mind reading. Too many family members assume your mind isn't in working order anyway. Explain your feelings. Show them your head isn't really empty.

7. District Attorneys belong in court. Leave the prosecutors on TV! Interrogation is for cross-examination-it will stop a conversation cold. A probing question and a demanding tone consistently bring On silence. If what you want is no response at all, demand one immediately.

8. Risk letting your family know the “real” you. There's a fifty percent chance they might like what you feel, think, say and do. You may hide yourself behind a shell. If you do, no one will ever be able to say' 'I like you for who you are.” Sure, it is frightening to reveal yourself to someone, but you stand a better chance of being accepted in your family.

9. No child has to be indulged, but don't forget you were

young once. You may now be much older and more sophisticated. Someone took the time to listen to you, answer your questions, show you a book, or hold you on his lap. Give a kid a break. Listen and let him pretend he is human too.

10. Don't just do something; act on what you feel. Touch each other with words or hands or both, being held closely may be the very best way to say "I know" or "I love you." Don't be afraid to touch, and don't be afraid to talk while you touch. The results might surprise you.

Somewhere I read that the five most important words a person can ever learn are: "I am proud of you." Those are extremely significant words because they contain simply a very complex truth: Everyone needs to be praised and feel appreciated. The family where appreciation is expressed not only toward its individual members but for its common and shared values has special strength. What they share expresses who they are together. For younger members of the family the activities and attitudes promoted within the life-style are subtle teachers of value.

When some children leave home they are told to "be good" while they are away. I remember hearing "be a good boy" many, many times. In our family we have developed a different approach. Often when our children have gone away for an activity, we have only said "remember what your name is." Occasionally, in joking situations, one member of the family will say, "if you are misbehaving, don't tell anyone your name." Or "don't tell anyone you belong to me when you act that way!" A guest in our home heard one of us say "remember what your name is" when our son left for an outing. It seemed natural for us, but for our guest it was as if someone had opened a door and let some light in. "Now I understand some of the reasons why your children behave nicely," she said. One thing every family shares is its name. Don't forget to express pride in yours.

In addition to parents saying they are proud of their children, teenagers can express pride in their parents. The list of things which can be elements of shared pride grows when you examine your lifestyle. Together you can have pride in your home, your church, your friends, your traditions, and many more. The more shared values the family experiences, either spoken or unspoken, the less room there will be for destructive conflicts.

As a student of Biblical history I have been fascinated by the concept of God and Israel as lovers. In the New Testament, Christ and the Church are called bride and groom. Believers are called a family of faith. Very early in church history Christians were called "followers of the way." The name grew not only because of persecution of Christians but also from their actions as they met together often and shared common experiences. Their rituals drew them together and their common faith was a mutual strengthening.

In a similar way, strong families share experiences, endure hardships together, and enjoy being with each other. One of the compliments to your family's life is when you or your children invite others to share it with you.

One of our family traditions has been to "expand" on holidays. Whenever possible we find someone who will not be with his family and invite him to share our holiday table and festivities. It has given us more for which to be thankful, and often made' us more aware of the true meaning of giving in these experiences.

Sharing is not just what a family does alike or together. It can also be what each member does individually and brings back to the family. “Do your own thing” is a good motto, but please share with us what you become as you do it. The single most repeated phrase I hear as a counselor is “I don't know him/her anymore.” It may be spoken by a husband, a wife, a parent, or a child. What it reflects can be a subtle drifting or a sudden change in a personality, but it represents an obvious division between people. The “plaintiff” feels left out of the “defendant's” life.

Strong families encourage individual creativity but maintain opportunities for sharing those experiences with each other. Every member expresses his uniqueness but enjoys it more by sharing it with his family. People learn to share themselves naturally in a family setting. If I do not learn how to share myself in my own family, I will have more difficulty learning to share myself outside my family.

Shakespeare said, “The saddest words of tongue or pen are these: it might have been.” How true! An Olympic boxer in 1976 won a gold medal two weeks after his mother's death. A popular ballad tells of a boy who played football better than ever because his blind father had died and from heaven could now see his son play for the first time. Morbidity is not my point; time is. I have seen many tears shed over lost opportunity within the family. Now is the time to express your love, to talk, to enjoy and to share with each other.

Take some quiet moments to reflect on the things your family has missed from your absence or what you would like to share with them. Make a list of those things and begin now to satisfy yourself by doing those things together.

What I have been doing is laying a foundation for the application of these principles of strong family life to money management. By now you can probably apply them for yourself. To get more family out of your dollar use your money to:

1. Express love.
2. Increase communication.
3. Enhance your intimacy.
4. Share time with each other:
5. Free each other for creativity.

Every family will have a unique way of implementing these principles, but no family will be poorer who really applies them! I dare you to become a rich family. The richer you are in relationships will be reflected in your decreasing money pressures. If you doubt it, test it. It will be worth it. If you have ever tried dieting, you know that the first few days are the hardest. You feel hungry and food is constantly on your mind. Then, gradually your appetite decreases as your body adjusts and you begin to lose pounds and gain satisfaction. To get more family out of your dollar will be a similar process. The first few efforts will probably bring increased tension and may even result in the overflow of buried feelings in the family.

Expect that - it is normal. Then, as you begin to make progress with united goals, you will discover much greater satisfaction in the use of these principles. Use your own wisdom and experiences to develop the five fundamental characteristics of strong family life.

TWO TESTS

Here are two yardsticks to measure your success. You can be sure you are applying the principles correctly when two facts exist in your family:

1. Each member appropriate to his age and experience understands and gives support to the resources, budget, and goals of the family.

2. Each member has some money with which to express his own personal freedom and for which he is accountable only to himself.

These principles become windows through which to look at how you are applying the "more" ideals to your family.

MUTUAL AGREEMENT

First, the parents are probably, though not in all cases, the major providers of income. If one member makes more money, he does not automatically gain more control. Where both parents work, a mutual disclosure of income and sharing of resources works best, Both husband and wife should have a complete understanding of the financial resources and commitments of the family, Both should be aware of the location of important documents such as deeds, insurance policies, wills, etc. (Parenthetically, both husband and wife should have a will. A simple handwritten sheet, witnessed by an adult other than your spouse is legal and satisfactory. But by all means, have a will, even if you don't think you need one.)

A single checking account is not necessary, but a unified budget is. Write down all your income and commitments. Agree on who will be responsible for what payments and how the balance of the income will be used. I have seen family money plans which ranged from complex 'multiple checking and savings accounts to a simple system in which weekly amounts of cash were placed in jars marked "rent," "car payment," etc. Both worked because all members of the family knew what the plan was and how it operated. Each person did his part to make it succeed.

The father, mother, and children need to understand and support the family's budget because it provides each of them with the best opportunity for personal freedom through the relationship.

PERSONAL FREEDOM

Not only parents but each child should get an "allowance" or some funds for which he alone is responsible. Within the family's budget system, he may create his own personal budget. Early in his life he may only use his money to buy a toy or some candy. Later he may want to make wider use of his choices as his allowance, and his own income, increases.

We taught our children to use the three divisions of money for themselves. Each learned to share, save, and spend. Because of our personal values each child was taught to give part of his allowance to the church, to put part in his savings account at the bank, and to spend whatever was left in any way he chose. These patterns learned in early childhood have persisted in their teen years.

As far as our family is concerned, the ancient Hebrew proverb is true: "Teach a child to choose the right path, and when he is older he will remain upon it."

TWELVE

USING YOUR FAMILY RESOURCES

"LORD, YESTERDAY I ASKED FOR ALL THINGS THAT I MAY ENJOY LIFE. TODAY, YOU GAVE ME LIFE THAT I MAY ENJOY ALL THINGS."

Ben Franklin reportedly said, "A man wrapped up in himself is the smallest package in the world." There is something crippling about limiting our experiences to one's self and one's world. Growth comes through conquering our immature selfishness and developing the mature selfhood that is ready to face others.

Getting more family out of your dollar is a growth goal. So far, we have. examined the needs, problems, and influences associated with the use of money. We have traced some different perspectives on finance, and have laid out a path for progress in relationships. The takeoff and flight have been exciting; now we land at our destination.

TOMORROW'S LEADERS

Families that get the most from their dollar give the world something in return – leadership for a new generation. A popular song says, "Teach the children of the world; they will be the parents of tomorrow."

Children are expensive. The cost of having a baby and providing for his basic needs through childhood, high school, college and into adult living has been estimated at a figure between $75,000.00 and 200,000.00. But I know few parents who are really satisfied with just "getting the child raised." Deep in the heart of most fathers and mothers is a desire to instill in their children sound principles which will see them through the stresses of growing up and survival both financially and emotionally.

Could it be that the true test of our child rearing is what our children will contribute to the world? Family "success" is difficult to define. There seems to be many more losers on the scene than winners. Parents have been and will continue to be judged on the results of their parenting as demonstrated through their children.

FULFILLING PARENTHOOD

What do we have to offer our children? Most children do not accept money as a substitute for the sharing of yourself. A good parent may leave his children a nice inheritance, bur this does not make a parent good. No man can be satisfied merely with the abundance of the things he gains. He is fulfilled instead by giving of himself.

My prosperity in life depends in large measure on my perspective. That perspective changes with my struggles in coping with daily pressures and accomplishments.

Someone has said that a "person is rich in proportion to the number of things he can afford to leave alone." Knowing what I do not need is as important as defining my needs. Unfortunately few of us see life that way. Instead, many of us have lessons about money that have to be "unlearned" before we can get the most out of family living.

LESSONS TO "UNLEARN"

Here are some common statements which reflect "poor parenting" in financial matters:

1. *It is important to have and hold money.* Wrong! Money is for using and exchanging, but not for hoarding. The desire to hoard is called greed.

2. *Money can buy anything or anybody* – everyone has his price. If I really believe this, I would have to own my world. Yet most of us experience the most important things in life as being free – a smile, a sunset, loving experiences. Other things-health, happiness, and security-are priceless and can't be bought.

3. *Rich people are better than poor people.* Some rich people-those who have a lot of money – have a lot of power, but only over material things. Since goodness is a quality, it cannot be measured quantitatively or purchased at any price.

4. *When you have money, you'll be happy!* Many of the world's richest people have been extremely unhappy. Happiness is usually the result of what you do with what you have rather than simply the amount you have.

5. *Spend your money today; you may not be here tomorrow.* Much immaturity and impulsivity have resulted

from this regrettable philosophy of relativism. One should be careful not to procrastinate - that is, to put off until tomorrow what he could do today. But equally important financially is that one should never sacrifice the permanent at the altar of the immediate!

I have heard these five statements numerous times in my counseling. They represent irrational thinking about money. How can we avoid teaching our children these and other limiting views of money and life?

CONSTRUCTIVE CHARACTERISTICS

I want to suggest to you several parental characteristics that I believe will help you develop in your children a more mature base for the use of money in living. Since how I use money in relationships teaches far more than what I say, these attributes must be seen experientially to be believed by my family. Effective relational living is learned through observing parents who have:

(1) ACCESSIBILITY

Parents who are open and available to their children "grow" better in their relationships. When it comes to money, children have questions to ask parents and other members of the family. Simple and sufficient responses to their inquiries takes some of the mystery out of money and builds a foundation for realism. Parents need to be accessible.

(2) ADAPTABILITY

The successful business is close to people and offers what they need. Parents who are good money models can adapt to the individuality of their children. To love someone is to give him room enough to grow. As each child matures, he will express his own uniqueness. Happy is the child who has adaptable parents!

(3) ABILITY

Poor managers make poor teachers. Being "rich and successful" doesn't necessarily reflect having ability with money. The man who can ably handle small amounts is almost always given more responsibility. Parents need only know the basic steps for management to be able instructors for their children. Your children need to see your capability demonstrated before they will accept your guidance.

(4) ACCURACY

Children learn the "laws" and "tables" of math. Practicing the basics is prerequisite to mastering them. Honest and accurate dealing with children creates more comfort within them for accurate money accounting on their own." impressing" your children by exaggerating costs or expenses will contribute to their losing faith in you and confusion regarding use of money.

(5) APPRECIATION

When your children express sound values monetarily or emotionally, they need recognition. The virtue of praise has been noted earlier. Politeness is a surface technique, but appreciation is a feeling for the sacrifice or efforts of another. The money value is not so important in a gift; appreciate the expression of caring that has been shown.

(6) AMBITION

Robert Browning said "A man's reach should exceed his

grasp." Often our goals reflect our feelings of confidence and worth. "Losers" – monetarily and emotionally – have low aims in life. "Winners" have a healthy restlessness with their accomplishments. Teach your children not to settle for anything less than their best.

(7) AUTHENTICITY

If you place people before things and the spiritual above the material, your children will be the first to know. If you don't, all your nicely articulated speeches will be wasted. The saying, "I would rather see a sermon any day than hear one," applies equally to financial lecturers. Sharing your struggles and your financial pressures makes you believable in the eyes of your children.

THE TEST OF TIME

Parenthood is a game in which only amateurs can compete. Because every child is different, we are rookies with each one of them. As Saul Minuchin clearly demonstrated the overall' 'family systems" is made up of subsystems composed of a network of one-co-one relationships.

Conflict and monetary distance are not signs of failure in the family; they represent the natural imbalances in the complex maze of multiple systems. The resources of the family are mobilized in troubled times to support each other through the crisis. In the face of an external challenge each supports the whole system, while in less strenuous times, family members may react more independently.

EMOTIONAL HEALTH

There are four signs of emotional maturity for individuals which may be applied to the family. If parents embody the attributes described earlier, the children and the family system will reveal:

1. A capacity to give and accept love.
2. An ability to establish and maintain appropriate behavioral limits.
3. A sense of identity and a perspective willing to accept feedback.
4. A willingness to face the mortality of the person or the system.

These marks of emotional maturity in a person or family can be specifically applied to the management of money. Getting more family out of your dollar is seen through:

1. A capacity to produce and expand your income in a unified and varied process which strengthens the individual members of the family and maintains the system.
2. An ability to establish and maintain credit sources and repay indebtedness while sharing a sense of balanced responsibility and freedom within the family budget.
3. A sense of pride in accomplishing together a common goal through a variety of specific plans.
4. A commitment to using the family resources inclusively not only for the needs of its members, but also for the needs of others through which the family can experience together an increased satisfaction.

When these basic principles are experienced in the family, the result is a reduction of money conflicts and an enhanced experience of sharing common goals and satisfactions.

The family is the basic unit of society. When families experience less tension together, there will be a dramatic effect on their views of the world.

Perhaps it will be a better place to live when we all learn how to get more family out of our dollar.

[1] *Saul Minuchin, Families and Family Therapy Cambridge, Mass.: Harvard University Press, 1974*

PART FIVE

WAYS TO USE THIS BOOK

"HOW COME THERE'S ALWAYS SO MUCH MONTH LEFT AT THE END OF THE MONEY?"

"I ONCE DREAMED OF THE DAY WHEN I'D BE EARNING THE SALARY I'M NOW STARVING ON."

You can read this book like any other book. You also have the option to get more involved. This can be done with your family or with a small group of other parents, or even by yourself. The questions that follow are designed to help you and/or your group expand on what you have read.

Each member of the family or of the group can start the discussion by stating what they expect to receive from these studies. There will be two parts to your expectation- what you want to share and what you hope to gain.

Encourage each member of your family or of the group to participate. If you are open about your thoughts and feelings, you will learn more about yourself, about others, and about the problems and pressures related to money. The objective is not to make anyone an authority on money, but to help cultivate better relationships within the family and encourage everyone to find their proper place of responsibility for the success of the family's financial situation.

Discord and disagreement is not a sign of failure or weakness. It can be a sign of strength. If the conflict is faced and worked on, the result will be a stronger relationship.

The questions which are included here are designed to be tools to help you enlarge the discussion of the concepts included in the book. They may help you to discover the root causes of your own lack of communication. Hopefully, you will be willing to consider all of the issues involved, but guard against getting involved in distracting tangents and losing the theme of your discussion.

If your time is limited, choose the questions or suggestions that are most appropriate to your family or group situation. We hope you will have a positive and refreshing experiences as you share your ideas and feelings with each other.

One caution: we do not expect you to become a therapy group. Asking helpful questions and making sure that you understand another's input will mean progress in sharing with each other. Demanding tones and probing questions will probably keep some members of your family or group from sharing with you. A good principle to keep in mind is that feelings are never right or wrong in and of themselves. Actions may be judged as having been right or wrong, but feelings simply are. What you feel exists-what you do with it may have "good" or "bad" results.

If you are using these questions in a group, be sure you read the guidelines for family and group discussion first.
Since this material will be used by many different families and by groups with different perspectives, the authors have tried to maintain broad but clear principles. We would be happy to have you send your comments for our research files to: Money Research, Suite 220, 1558 Marietta Hwy, Canton, Georgia 30114.

GUIDELINES FOR FAMILY AND GROUP DISCUSSION

The purpose of family or small group discussions is to facilitate personal growth through meaningful relationships. These guidelines will enhance your learning experience. Leaders of the group should share some of these ideas with the group.

1. Participate; don't just observe.

2. Accept and encourage expressions of feeling.

3. Avoid confusion. Focus on the process of communication. Don't try to analyze.

4. Sit in a circle or informal setting. Be comfortable, open and flexible.

5. Avoid deadlock questions. Try to clarify these with specific practical applications or illustrations.

6. Assign "homework" based upon the conclusion of the discussion. Implementation by assuming responsibility for change is essential.

7. Individuals can learn, grow and change if they share and work together. You can encourage that process.

8. Stay on the subject. Avoid pursuing tangents.

9. Clarify what is being said through reflection, feedback, self-disclosure and redefinition.

10. If you feel someone is monopolizing or controlling the group, then share your concern.

11. Let silence be your friend. If necessary, restate the question casually.

12. Acknowledge any contribution in an honest, genuine manner. Appreciate the person's effort to contribute.

13. If someone asks a question, allow others in the group an opportunity to answer before you do.

14. When you get a "wrong answer" or deadlock statement, say' 'I'm wondering how the rest of you feel about that" or "what other ideas do the rest of you have about that."

15. A group leader" models" behavior for his group. They will "grow" no further than you do.

QUESTIONS FOR CHAPTER I: IMPROVING FAMILY LIFE- IS IT POSSIBLE WITHOUT MORE MONEY?

1. The key words and ideas found in this chapter are money, more, family and improving. Can money create happiness? In what respect?

2. Why does money not always bring security, happiness or increased family togetherness?

3. How does the lack of financial resources also create conflict?

4. In some circumstances could a lack of sufficient funds be a worthwhile learning experience or benefit for a family?

5. What are the subtle messages and pressures that advertising media convince us of?

6. Discuss the financial fantasy that "quantity equals quality."

7. When can financial success become a blinder to one's own personal worth, values, and motivations?

8. Focus on the 4 "More" Principles outlined in this chapter.

a. Consider why it is important to set goals in your family that are related to getting "more family" out of your dollar.

b. What does it mean to get more family out of the family's dollar?

c. Describe a childhood memory which reflects the goals or values you have learned directly or indirectly from your family's attitudes, activities or conversations.

d. How much time should a mother and father allow for their vocation or profession? How can one's obligation to their job subtly eat away at family development and responsibilities?

e. What can the other extreme of no concern for financial stability and increase do to the family growth process?

f. What kinds of family interactions best teach children the value of money and how it should be used?

g. Why does more money management teach responsibility? What kinds of freedoms result when financial controls are designed for the benefit of family relationships?

9. What kind of relationships with others bring real satisfaction in life? How can you discern the proper use of your time and money in order to get more effective and meaningful relationships in your family experience?

10. Have each person list 3 goals for your family. Share those goals and together list 5 priority goals you can agree upon as a group.

11. What basic values are underlying the above goals?

12. Establish specific procedures and activities in which your family can participate together In order to experience the above values and goals.

QUESTIONS FOR CHAPTER II: YOUR MONEY TALKS-WHAT DOES IT SAY?

Determining your priorities: ,
1. State five priorities for living. Share what you want to accomplish in these five areas.

2. Next, indicate how much time and money you invest in your daily activities for each of these objectives.

3. What are the values underlying these priorities in investments of time and money? What is your money (and your use of it) saying about you?

4. What childhood experiences and memories do you recall that reveal some of your present attitudes toward money?

5. How do you use money? What are some of the ways others choose to use money? Compare and contrast the positive and negative uses of money. How many of your suggestions are centered on developing family intimacy and relationships? What is your money saying about your family?

QUESTIONS FOR CHAPTER III: YOUR PATTERNS GUIDE¬HOW DO THEY LEAD?

1. What kind of saving habits would you like to see in your children now and when they are on their own? What values are taught by these habits? How can you model these habits?

2. Share with your group what your greatest temptations are when it comes to overspending the budget.

3. Why do many persons fail to evaluate their spending patterns and follow a fixed budget? In what way might that attitude be related to our fear of examining our personal value systems?

4. Do the experiment suggested in the chapter with your family and share the results with them. Now begin to determine new guidelines together as to how you could spend, save, and share your resources for the next three months.

5. Reflect and share some experiences in your life in which another person's generosity brought unexpected benefit and blessing to you and others.

QUESTIONS FOR CHAPTER IV: FAMILY INTERACTION LESSONS

Make a graffiti poster. A graffiti poster represents many different ideas and opinions about an assigned subject. It allows for interaction and discovery learning through involvement with each other in small groups.

Directions: Take two large pieces of blank paper, newsprint, or poster board and tape it to a wall (a blackboard and chalk could also be used). Ask each person to take a magic marker or large felt tip pen and begin writing words, phrases, and pictures which describe for him/her (a) what is a family? List both positive and negative characteristics or descriptions. On the second poster (b) what kinds of interactions, relationships, and communication exchanges take place in families? Some are not so obvious or visible, so think deeply.

Each person may share his own ideas or confer with the other members in the group before writing or drawing his response. When you are finished, step back and share and discuss what you as a group have become aware of about the communication and interaction process within the family.

QUESTIONS FOR CHAPTER V: AITITUDES SEND MESSAGES

It is important to understand how messages are sent and received in a family. The paths of communication are not just part of a family system but are the essential component of it.

1. Have your family or group sit in a circle with a pile of old magazines. Have each person leaf through the magazines and tear out five pictures each which visualize the kinds of messages people send about themselves or about others. Find at least two of the descriptions mentioned in Chapter V (resentment, resignation, rigidity and rebellion). These can depict persons who are blamers, those who show helplessness, control, or revenge.

2. Show the pictures you chose to the group and tell why you chose these particular scenes. Share with the group the kinds of feelings and reactions you have when you meet these kinds of people. List both positive and negative messages and feelings.

3. What are you communicating to those around you through your attitude about money? What message would you like to have your money give about you?

QUESTIONS FOR CHAPTER VI: MONEY MANAGEMENT MIRRORS

Take each of the character descriptions in Chapter VI and discuss the following:

1. How does the principle of reflection help you to gain insight into the cause of your money problems?

2. What attitudes toward yourself and money must change in order to solve your money conflicts?

3. How can your understanding toward others open up new insights for you and your family relationships?

4. Brainstorm together and develop a list of "homework assignments" for the group to work on and to share together.

QUESTIONS FOR CHAPTER VII: LEARN YOUR FINANCIAL ABC'S

1. Determine what system is operating in your family philosophy of money:

a. Identify the feelings and attitudes toward buying which cause conflict in your marriage or family.

b. What system controlled the marriage and family in which you were reared? How does your family background and values influence your decision today?

2. Awareness is the first key word in the ABC Plan. Identify some of the reasons why you spend money.

3. The second word is balance. Do the suggested exercise in the ABC Plan. Begin to determine your new "compromise budget". In what way will this allow for everyone to participate in the process of earning the family income and resources? How will it create family unity? You may want to choose a specific area to consider in your financial plan, such as planning for a vacation, buying seasonal tickets for a family fun time, developing a savings program, or buying a new car.

4. The third word is commitment. Identify your competitive goals. What other benefits can you imagine from a relationship based on the illustration given about Bill and Jackie?

QUESTIONS FOR CHAPTER VIII: POWER FOR THE PLASTIC PIT

1. What ways have you seen others "financing their loneliness"?

2. Based upon this chapter, discuss the pros and cons of using credit. As a group, write a set of guidelines which would be helpful in avoiding credit pitfalls.

3. Discuss ways you might apply the principle found in Dr. Schuller's story entitled, "Never Borrow Money For Coal".

QUESTIONS FOR CHAPTER IX: KEEP WHAT YOU GIVE AWAY

1. How are your values about life and family relationships expressed in your use of money?

2. When does money become your master?

3. Why is it more beneficial to give people priority over things? In what ways do we often violate this principle even though we may give lip service to it?

4. Share your opinions and responses to the "Five Affirmations of Priceless Personhood".

5. Discuss the statement "As you extend yourself through giving, you gain priceless treasures that can never be taken away".

QUESTIONS FOR CHAPTER X: HANDLING FAMILY MONEY CONFLICTS

1. Identify the various kinds of power struggles you see in family conflicts today.

2. Why do families argue over money?

3. Based upon the ideas in this chapter, outline a list of "rules for solving money conflicts".

4. Why are listening skills important in solving money conflicts? Share with your group what it means for someone to listen to you. What listening skills need to be learned in your family?

QUESTIONS FOR CHAPTER XI: LEARNING PRACTICAL CONCEPTS TOGETHER

1. What are the prevailing characteristics that describe the kind of "family atmosphere" in your family? Compare them to the list in Chapter 11.

2. Review each of the 10 points on improving family conversations and communication. Which ones are missing in your family? Why? What can you begin to do about improving in these areas?

3. How can your family become 'richer', in its relationships?

4. What does it mean to have "personal freedom" in the family's budget system? How will these principles help everyone to grow into responsible "earners, savers and spenders"?

QUESTIONS FOR CHAPTER XII: USING YOUR FAMILY RESOURCES

1. Discuss the author's statements, “a person is rich in proportion to the number of things he can afford to leave alone,” and “knowing what I do not need is as important as defining my needs”.

2. Which of the five “lessons to unlearn” are most prominent in your family? How can you begin to “unlearn” them?

3. Review briefly each of the seven principles of effective relational living. Discuss those that are most meaningful to you.

4. Explore together the nature of family interaction which encourages openness in family sharing. What signs of emotional maturity are lacking today in our families?

5. Discuss the quote, “Lord, yesterday I asked for all things that I may enjoy life. Today you gave me life that I may enjoy all things.” Why can we never be fully satisfied merely with the abundance of the things we have?

Let's talk about money. Specifically, your money and how to make it do what you want it to do.

Face it, it's not just a case of income-because no matter how much you make, you're never going to have enough money for everything. So, to make the best use of what you have, you need a money management plan.

If you're like most people, the idea of working out a plan of money management doesn't come at the top of your list of “fun” things to do. You probably think of it as budgeting-cutting out all the things you enjoy. Don't. Think of a money management plan as a way to stretch your dollars, to accomplish the goals you've set, and to prevent many financial problems that might pop up unexpectedly.

First, let's find out how you feel about money. Sure, you like it-but that's not the point. The thing you have to decide is what money really means to you. It's really a question of attitude. Maybe you want to use it to enjoy the present. Or perhaps you' d rather live fairly modestly now and save some for the future. Money means different things to different people. There's no such thing as “right” and “wrong” in spending, as long as you realize that buying one thing may mean giving up something else-and as long as you can afford what you buy.

After deciding how you want to use your money, the next step is to set your goals.

Generally speaking, you should consider two different types of goals: short-range and long-range. Short-range goals might be next year's vacation or something you know you'll have to buy in just a few years, such as a new car or a major appliance. Long-range goals are for more distant planning - college for your children, a new home, or retirement income.

A tip: be sure to establish goals you can reach. Be realistic about your income, and don't set your sights on things you really can't afford. If you do, you'll just become discouraged and give up.

Jot down your goals and then go on to figure out how to reach them.

With your goals set, your next step is to see where you now stand financially.

Start by taking a good look at your assets. Be sure to include everything; you may be surprised to find you have more than you think. The worksheet at the back of this booklet, a "Balance Sheet," will help provide a guide.

Put down your checking and savings accounts, government bonds, and the current value of any investments. If you own a car or a home, write down their present market value. And don't forget to add other personal property-anything with a potential resale value. Also, on the asset side, list the present cash value of your life insurance.

Now comes the unpleasant part: figuring out what you owe. Write down the amount of your outstanding loans, mortgages, charge accounts and any other debts.
By subtracting your liabilities from your total assets, you get a picture of your net worth.

ASSETS
Checking account Savings account
U.S. Government Bonds Life insurance cash values Investments
House
Other real estate Annuities
Company or union pension Interest in business Automobile
Personal property
Other
LIABILITIES
Installment loans Other loans Charge accounts Mortgage
Other debts
TOTAL NET WORTH
(Subtract total liabilities from total assets to get net worth)

EMERGENCY FUND
Emergency fund goal is amount to be put into fund weekly, biweekly or monthly
LIVING EXPENSES
(Weekly, biweekly or monthly estimates) _
Food
Clothing
Household expenses (maintenance, laundry, cleaning, etc.)
Transportation
Entertainment and recreation
Regular medical and dental expenses Personal care items and allowances
Other
TOTAL LIVING EXPENSES SUMMARY
TOTAL WEEKLY, BIWEEKLY OR MONTHLY INCOME
TOTAL WEEKLY, BIWEEKLY OR MONTHLY OUTGO (Total "set aside" for fixed expenses plus amount for emergency fund plus total living expenses)
BALANCE
For regular savings, investments or special goal (Subtract outgo from income to get balance)

How does it look? Do you need to make some changes in spending habits so you'll have more to add to your assets? Should you _ figure out ways to accumulate more money for future security? Keep these questions in mind as you go about setting up a plan.

You can also make a list of your personal resources.
People often overlook these assets, yet your skills and your personal characteristics-such as dependability, energy, and ability to work well with people-are valuable assets that can help you reach your goals.

And remember-your personal resources can be increased, just as money assets can . Your talents can be polished and expanded to improve your chances for advancement in your present job or to prepare you for a new job. You may be able to do this by attending night school or adult education classes.

The key to workable money management is planning. And it's important to do your planning on two levels:
•A plan for day-to-day or month-to-month spending .
•A plan for accumulating financial resources for emergencies and long-range financial security.

You'll also want to study all the various consumer tools and buying methods available to you to decide which suit your needs best. These are discussed later.

Setting up a plan isn't the end. In a way, it's the beginning. You'll have to stick to it, evaluate it as you go along, and-if necessary-revise it.

Now you're ready to get down to the nitty-gritty: developing a spending plan to suit your needs. The worksheet, the "Financial Plan," should help you set it up. This you do in six steps ...

First, add up your total income. If you're going to use your money wisely, you have to know just how much you have to work with. Your money sources may come from a job, insurance benefits, pension payments, Social Security or investments. Write down exactly what you will receive annually from every source.

When figuring money from work, be sure to put down only the amount of your take-home pay-not your gross salary. There's quite a difference after Federal and State withholding taxes, Social Security taxes, group insurance premiums and union dues have been deducted. Although some of your deductions may be going into savings or insurance-group life or health insurance or a retirement annuity, for example-don't include them in your money plan. You're working out a plan for the dollars you have for spending.

Don't forget to add other sources of income: interest from savings accounts, dividend payments from stock or life insurance, or a Christmas bonus, if you're sure you'll be getting one.

If you work part-time, or on a commission basis, or free-lance work, use an average income figure.

And if your family has more than one wage earner, include all take home pay in adding up the total Income.

Now figure your total fixed expenses. How much do you need for rent or mortgage payments, insurance premiums, car payments, church or other contributions, telephone and utility bills? Write these figures down. Include an estimate for income tax, too, if it is not withheld.

Don't guess. You need exact amounts for best results. Gather up your receipts and look through your cancelled checks and try to see exactly where- your money went last year.

You'll notice that some of your fixed expenses come due annually and others, monthly or weekly. Your best bet is to figure everything out on an annual basis. Then, by adding them all together, you can see how many dollars to set aside regularly to be sure you have the money on hand when payments come due.

It's up to you-and maybe the timing of your paycheck-to select which time period is best for you: weekly, biweekly or monthly. Depending on which you choose, you can divide the annual total by 52, 26, or 12. This will tell you the amount you have to set aside regularly. This “set aside” principle is a key factor in making your “money plan” work.

Next, determine your day-to-day living expenses.

This includes food, clothing, transportation, entertainment, routine medical and dental care, household expenses, and personal allowances for each member of your family. If you can't pin clown your actual costs, you may have to estimate them at first. Then, if necessary, you may want to keep a record of expenses for three months or so to get a clearer picture of what you actually are spending for day-co-day living.

You'll need a savings fund to handle emergencies and achieve special goals. It will help carry you over a financial crisis if your car or refrigerator breaks down unexpectedly or some great opportunity comes along. It will also keep you from dipping into the dollars you've set aside for daily living, or taking out a loan or selling investments to cover these emergencies.

Start your savings fund by setting aside a fixed amount regularly-no matter how small-until you've reached the total you need for your emergency fund. As a guide, you might decide to keep a certain percentage of your income or expenses in this fund.

If there's any money left over, see how you might use it to increase your assets. To determine this, add together your fixed and day-to-day items and your emergency fund amount, then subtract the total from the income you've worked out in Step One. The remaining dollars loan be put toward additional savings, or investments.

If there isn't money left over, go over your spending plan again. Can you reduce some of your day-to-day items? Take a really close look at your "fixed" costs. You may be surprised to discover that you can economize on some of them, too.

Don't be discouraged if your plan doesn't work out exactly right the first time. And even when you've developed a working plan, you should review it from time to time to make sure it's in line with your current income and expenses.

Remember, a spending plan is a helpful guide, not a rigid, inflexible rule. You can always adjust it or even start over if the plan is not working to suit you. And keep in mind that you don't always have to spend the same amount in each area, except where an expense cannot be reduced. For example-, you may decide to cut down on entertainment for a time to save toward a special vacation.

Now Your money management plan is all set up. But to keep it working smoothly, you need to consider the various consumer tools available to you ...

Yes. Your money management plan should have some type of savings to provide readily available cash in case of emergencies and as a means of meeting future needs and reaching goals. This can be done through an account in a bank, savings and loan association or credit union. All pay interest on your money.

A word about interest: the rate can make a difference, especially when interest is compounded when interest is paid on interest-over a period of time. This is true even if it's only a fraction of one percent. The more often that interest is compounded during a year, the more your savings grow. For instance, a bank that compounds interest daily, rather than quarterly, lets your savings grow faster. So compare interest rates when you're trying to decide on a place to save money.

Let's look at the different choices available to you:

• Commercial banks (also called full-service banks) offer you the widest range of services. In addition to savings accounts, they provide checking accounts, make various types of loans (auto, mortgage, personal and business) and many of them handle family estates, trusts and investments.

• Savings banks generally pay higher interest rates than commercial banks, but offer different services. However, not all states have savings banks, so be sure to check it out.

• Savings and loan associations generally pay higher interest on deposits than commercial banks, but do not provide the same range of services.

• Credit unions aren't banks, as such. They're usually associations whose members have a common bond, such as place of employment, professional association, or union membership. Credit unions receive savings and make personal loans to members. Technically, members do not make deposits; they purchase shares. Credit unions do handle checking accounts. Interest rates vary, but are generally among the lowest available.

• U.S. Savings Bonds are popular with many people who like the payroll deduction feature available through most businesses. You can also purchase them directly at your bank. There are two types-Series E and Series H-and both pay the same rate of interest. With Series E bonds, the tax on the interest is not payable until you cash them. So if you hold the bonds until retirement, when your income is lower, your tax will also be lower. Interest on Series H bonds is paid semiannually and is taxable in that year.

• Certificates of deposit are another type of savings tool also available at your bank. Here you purchase a certificate in a given amount for an agreed-upon length of time. In return, you get a higher rate of interest than the bank's savings accounts. Before investing in certificates of deposit, however, you should be sure you will not need to cash them in before they mature, because you will lose part of your interest as a penalty if you do.

How much money should you keep in a savings account? That's a hard question to answer. Although some financial experts advise the equivalent of two months to six months income, the real decision is yours to make-based upon your needs.

If you're like most people, at some time or another an opportunity or emergency will come your way at a time when you're Iowan money . You won't be able to handle it without using credit or taking out a loan.

Don't despair. It's not always possible to pay cash for everything. However, keep in mind that it's likely to cost you extra, because you'll have to pay interest on the money you borrow and on most credit plans, as well.

Remember that you'll have to pay off these charges and loans, so use caution. Careless use of credit can sink you deeply into debt, and rising prices in the future could put a squeeze on your budget and make payments hard to meet.

Basically, there are five types of loans:

•Passbook and life insurance loans are perhaps the least expensive of all. With the first type, you must have money in the bank; with the second, you must own a life insurance policy with cash value. With a bank passbook loan, your savings are held by the bank as collateral, but continue to earn interest. If you fail to repay the loan, of course, the bank takes the money from your account.

In the case of a life insurance loan, you can borrow against the cash value that has built up in your policy, and the interest rate is moderate. The interest rate that you will pay is written into your policy . You can repay the loan whenever you choose to do so.

However, this type of loan has a danger. If you don't repay it, and you should die while the loan is in effect, the amount you've borrowed, plus any interest still due, will be subtracted from the insurance proceeds before it is paid to your beneficiary.

• Installment loans means that part of the loan must be repaid every month.

• Single-payment loans are just what they sound like: a loan you must repay completely at one time.

There are two kinds: demand loans, which means you have to repay the loan when the lender asks for it, and time loans, which means you have to pay the entire sum at a pre-set maturity date. Usually you'll have to put up collateral, such as stock or bonds, for a single-payment loan.

• Second mortgages can be taken out with your home as collateral to provided needed money. In other words, in addition to the first mortgage which -you took out to finance your home purchase, you take out a second mortgage for a stated period of time. Although you usually can raise money quickly and spread your payments over a long period, taking out a second mortgage is an expensive way to borrow money, since the interest rates are high.

• Credit card loans are one of the fastest ways to borrow money, because you use your previously-established credit to get the loan. However, you will probably have to pay a high rate of interest in return. Credit card loans use a "revolving credit" arrangement. Interest-usually between 12 and 18 percent per year-is applied to the unpaid balance of your loan. Because credit card loans are so easy, you'll want to be careful not to overuse them.

Where should you go to get a loan? Overall, the best place is your bank. Although some other places may seem easier, your bank will probably offer the lowest costs and fairest terms for most purposes.

Of course, you might also be able to borrow from a member of your family at little or no interest with flexible repayment arrangements.

Location of will ________________________________

Location of insurance policies ______________________

Location of investment certificates __________________

Location of other important papers __________________

Social Security number ___________________________

Checking account number and bank _________________

Savings account number and bank __________________

Safe deposit box number and bank __________________

Others ____

CPSIA information can be obtained at www.ICGtesting.com
Printed in the USA
LVOW122251141112

307396LV00002B/1/P

9 781936 815647